P9-CRK-805

don't stand too close to a naked man

TIM ALLEN

don't stand too close to a naked man

HYPERION
NEW YORK

Copyright © 1994 Boxing Cat Productions, Inc.

Illustrations copyright © 1994 Mary Lee Hannington.

All rights reserved. No part of this book may be used or reproduced in any man-
ner whatsoever without the written permission of the Publisher. Printed in the
United States of America. For information address Hyperion, 114 Fifth Avenue,
New York, New York 10011.

Library of Congress Cataloging-in-Publication Data
Allen, Tim, 1953–
    Don't stand too close to a naked man / Tim Allen. — 1st ed.
        p.   cm.
    ISBN 0-7868-6134-7
    1. Men—Humor. I. Title. II. Title: Do not stand too close to a
naked man
    PN6231.M45A37   1994
    818'.5402—dc20   94-28625
                                                                  CIP

Designed by Claudyne Bianco

FIRST EDITION

10 9 8 7 6 5 4 3 2 1

FOR LAURA AND KADY.

FOR THE FATHER AND GRANDFATHERS I MISS; AND FOR MY NEW DAD, BILL,
WHO STEPPED UP TO THE PLATE AND HIT A HOME RUN FOR ALL OF US.

AND MOST OF ALL, FOR HAVING ME, FOR MOM.

CONTENTS

ACKNOWLEDGMENTS

All men like to think they can do it alone, but a real man knows there's no substitute for good help, support, encouragement, or a pit crew.

So, special thanks to David Rensin for helping me make sense of my thoughts and memories, for patience at the right times, and most of all for teaching me how to use my modem.

Also, thanks to:

Kim "Bacca" Flagg, for her brilliant left and right hooks.

All of my siblings, especially Becky, Geoff, and Steve, for their notes.

The people on the set of the film, *The Santa Clause,* for putting up with me finishing my first book during the filming of my first movie.

Leslie Wells at Hyperion.

Peg and Mia.

Bobby Click and a nice letter from the past.

Apologies to everyone I had to "kill" in print.

And to all the people in my life for making my life something worth writing about—although I think I also had something to do with it.

If I've forgotten *anyone*, it's only because I'm totally egocentric. If I'd had *my* way, I would have dedicated this book to myself and told everyone else to go straight to . . .

don't stand too close to a naked man

INTRODUCTION:
the naked truth

This book is about many things I want to say about being a man. If you've seen my comedy act or my television show, or me in the shower, it will explain why the book is not about many things I want to say about being a woman.

At first, I didn't want to write this. Don't get me wrong: I like books, I read a lot. I know lots of great authors' names. I can spell "Camille Paglia." It's just that when you're working television, movies, and the stage you want to use your spare time for lots of things that seem more important than writing. Seeing my wife and child more than twice a year comes immediately to mind. Plus I didn't think it would be fair if I didn't write the book myself. So I put it off for a long time.

The publisher finally took some drastic measures, which convinced me that being an author would be a wise addition to my résumé. Here's what changed my mind about doing the book.

Hyperion is owned by Disney, which also owns my television show. Disney owns Disneyland and Disney World. Disney also owns Euro-Disney, Tokyo-Disney, and a Disney store in every city, town, and hamlet in the world. *They also have my cat.*

First things being first, we needed a title, I came up with *Don't Stand Too Close to a Naked Man.* I'm not sure what it means—or if I want to know what it means—but I knew it was a winner when the mere mention of it made several people shoot pricey mineral water through their noses.

This book will be like my taking you for a spirited ride in my 575-horsepower Mustang. We go where I want, see the things I like. When we really get moving you will have to trust me, since it's the first time I've driven this thing. Also, I'm a very goal-oriented guy. So I'm hoping that by the end of this book you will not only have thought more about men, and what makes a man a man, as well as about how men and women relate, but you'll also have learned to speak Spanish, cook a soufflé, rebuild a Hemi, and remove blood-stains from white shirts.

The truth is that writing is a challenge. It's great to see your stuff in print. I also desperately wanted to see the words "fart lighting" and "sack" on a page.

Bottom line—we're getting close to the bottom, aren't we?—I'm a man and I've arrived at that juncture in life when it's time to share what I've learned. It's been an interesting journey. Hell, it *took* forty years. So much is happening to guys today, from the women's movement to changing social values to the demise of the Sears catalog. This book is about how I got to where I am before this book ended my career. It probably has a few things to say about how you men got to where you are, too. And it will give the ladies a look into secret corners that men rarely discuss, much less sweep up regularly.

And if all goes well and you buy lots and lots of copies, maybe Disney will give me back my cat.

my name
made me
do it

Even though we've never met, I want you to know *right now* how much I admire you. You're the greatest.

"Admire *me*?" you're saying. "Thanks. But why?"

Easy. In this era of declining literacy, you're reading a book. Actually *reading* a book. I'm so impressed.

Of course, it's *my* book, which *really* makes you special. After all, I'm a guy best known for grunting and blowing up toasters, not writing. *I* know there's much more to me, but *you* took a chance. You trusted me.

So I'm going to trust *you*.

See, I have something to tell you. I've got to let it out and let it go. Unload. Own up. Confess. I just can't hold back any longer. . . .

I'm a Dick. Yes. I *am* a Dick. My closest friends know I'm a Dick. In fact, my brothers are Dicks, my cousins are Dicks, and my sister—before she was married—was a Dick. My dad? One incredible Dick, and the Dick responsible for *me* being a Dick. Timothy Allen Dick. My given name, and a gift to cherish for a lifetime.

Some of us are just born lucky.

My name almost got me kicked out of a restaurant once. After I'd politely told the hostess, "Dick, party of six," she said, "Excuse me?" like I'd offended her. I said, "What's the problem? I'm Mr. Dick, and it's a party of six." Her face tightened with contempt, and she said, "Really, sir. I don't have to take this." "*Take* this?" I was getting (tired of dickering?) ticked off. I said, "Lady, you got a problem with Dicks? I've been a Dick all my life. I'd like to see you be a Dick for just one day!" The hostess was about to signal the manager when my wife spoke up. "Excuse me, miss," she said, sweetly. "My husband's correct. He *is* a Dick. Which, I guess, makes me a Dick, too." For a moment, she let that hang in the air, then added, "Now what about that table?"

The hostess grabbed six menus and seated us in the smoking section. It isn't easy being a Dick.

Now I know what you're wondering: How, where, when, and why would he do something like lose the Dick, and was it on an out-patient basis? I'll never forget that moment. When I did my first TV talk show, the producers said they just didn't feel comfortable flashing my real name onscreen. "Surely you understand, Tim—Dick? People will think you made it up just to be funny." I wished I had. I wanted to be a comedian so much. But I relinquished the Dick to keep my spot on their show. The separation hurt less than I thought it would. And so began the career of Tim Allen.

But why am I even telling you this? A couple of reasons.

First, I believe my name created my life. Dealing from childhood with people's reactions helped form the basis of my humor about men and the differences between men and women. All my life, no one ever failed to remind me that my name is synonymous with the slang for penis. It's no wonder my self-image is so closely tied to that organ.

Second, and most poignant, I've always wanted to see the sentence "I'm a Dick" in print. But then, haven't we all?

(For some reason, right now, I feel . . . oh, never mind. It's silly. Well—okay. I'm feeling very close to you, and yet kind of vulnerable.)

As an experiment, I'm going to use words like "dick" and "penis" here and there. It's not to be rude or offensive. They're just words. The symbols and meanings—positive, negative, enlightening, insulting—are in our heads, which is why the power of some words has a lot to do with all the social and sexual dysfunction in this country. What I learned growing up is that we have power over words, not the other way around. People made fun of my name every day, but I learned to cope. I numbed myself. Maybe I can pass my immunity on to you.

It's okay. I've been tested.

What's in a name? Interesting question to ponder. It depends on your point of view. A scholar might say that words or groups of words define our identities. The head of a successful corporation might say a name contains the power of association and reputation. I haven't really given it much thought. So let's see—what's in a name? I know. Maybe it's an endless cycle of excruciating torture causing tremendous pain and misery to a young boy who is knocked to his knees time and time again and made to suffer hell on earth merely because he is bound to a name that, when uttered, universally conjures up the image of male genitalia (specifically, the penis), and results in snickers and jeers from evil little children, who so easily find amusement in cruelty, and who so relish the poor boy's anguish, shame, and humiliation that he's left only to mutter the words "character building? character building, my ass," over and over like some escaped lunatic.

Or maybe it's just a collection of vowels and consonants.

Not that it ever bothered me. As a kid, all I had to do was say, "Hi, I'm Tim Dick," and I already knew that people saw me as a walking penis.

To this day I'm not exactly sure *why* it's so funny to everyone. Given the male organ's important role in society, and men and women's fondness for "it," you'd think that, instead of being teased, I'd be revered. The Carnegies of Pittsburgh. The Rockefellers of New York. The Dicks of Denver. I should have been a deity in high school. Girls should have sought out my advice, stood in line to date me. I should have been given the key to the city. (By the way, it's not too late for that.)

Tim Dick. Tin Dick. Thin Dick. Pin Dick. And then there's my Uncle Richard—a double Dick. And he named his son Peter. Nice.

In grade school the kids snickered at my name the same way they giggled when they had to sing the word "bosom" in "The Battle Hymn of the Republic."

When I was older, my gym teachers—who clearly wished they were still in the Marines—*always* paused at my name.

In class, I knew the alphabet better than anybody. And I feared whosoever name came before mine, especially on the first day of school. I can still feel the old heartburn and anxiety. "Aaron, Becker, Bendleston, Cochran, Dachman, Decker, DICK!" It seemed like the guy was yelling it through a megaphone. The whole class would stop talking, and everybody would stare at me like I resembled my name.

The guys in high school were relentless.

"What's your name?"

"Tim Dick."

"Dick! Hahaha! Like Penis? Hahaha!" I wasn't just going to stand there and take it, so I'd have to run through a whole routine just to defuse the situation. When they'd say, "Your dad shoulda called you Harry," I could mouth the words along with my tormentors. I'd go, "Oh, wow, Harry. You should be a comedian. Harry. Real original! I've never heard that one. How about Big? That's a fine Irish name! Lotsa guys named Big. How about Thick? You're a funny guy!"

For a while I hated everyone and the teasing caused me unnecessary grief. But in retrospect, it made me a better person. Now I have to *thank* my name for making my life special. This wouldn't have happened if I were Tim Dack, or Tim Deck, or Tim Dock.

Maybe Tim Cock, though.

After graduation, just when I thought I'd been through it all, I met a woman in a sporting-goods store where I worked. She was mature and had six kids. Out of nowhere she said, "Too bad you don't have a sister named Anita."

Anita Dick. Now *that* is really funny.

When you're a kid you never really call what you've got by its real name. Anything but that. Dicks were big in my family—naturally. Then there's boner, chubby, Hank, pecker, willy, Mr. Happy, pocket rocket, trouser trout, joystick, and "it." There are millions of synonyms. Of course, my all-time favorite is Big Sam and the Twins. Go figure.

Women have names for it, too.

But they won't tell us.

You can say "penis" in front of your parents. Otherwise, we use the word only when speaking medically. Doctors say, "I have to see your penis," which sounds like you need to get something lanced. My doctor calls it a "unit." I don't argue. I've seen how he holds his golf club.

When you're a boy, the penis is mostly a yardstick by which to measure growth.

I remember the first time I saw my dad's. He, my brothers, and I were gathered in the bathroom. Then I looked at it. I have no idea why—maybe because I was just waist-high—and it was the most shocking thing I'd ever seen. It was so frightening that I swore I would never want anything like that in all my life. I now know that you have to be careful what you wish for.

"Vagina" is a funny word. Almost as funny as "penis." I always stumble over it—I mean the word. Va-gi-na. Women don't even use the word. I know one woman who uses "ginnie." Ginnie is more personable, I guess.

I say this all in the most respectful way, you understand. Since I have a daughter, I have to teach her what to call it, and it can't be "down there"—the name I cleverly created—all her life. One reason I think we get so screwed up is not calling things by the right name.

So: A man has a penis. A woman has a boom-ba. Okay, I'll be honest, she's got a goo-goo. I don't know why this is so difficult. My daughter already calls it a butty-butt. I said, "You have, as you well know, a butty-butt." But she calls everything in that area a butty-butt.

Please tell me this will pass.

My daughter also has major questions about why I can pee standing up. She automatically assumes it's a better deal. *I* didn't say anything, but who knows what she hears at school. So I said, "No, you're lucky. You get to sit." She goes, "When I grow up I'll be able to pee standing up." I thought, that'd be interesting. I feel bad for women. They have to go through such a to-do to go to the bathroom. And they can't write their names in the snow without a lot of acrobatics.

Before we figure out that we can play doctor, we rely on sex-education films, science books, and that old standby *National Geographic*, to reveal what we've got . . . down there.

Those medical illustrations are pretty weird, aren't they? The man is cross-sectioned so that you get a limp side view. And women are cut along an axis between front and back, which makes their internal reproductive system look like there's a water buffalo trapped inside. Or an inverted penis. After seeing those diagrams, I actually believed that if a woman blew on her thumb hard enough, she would have what I have—that it would just pop out.

This was all very confusing when I was a kid. My dad died when I was young. Although my mom was very good about explaining the birds and bees, whenever my brothers and I would ask about how the male and female actually got together, it was suddenly dinnertime. Since then, the smell of home cooking always makes me feel silly and sexy.

The penis is an emotional organ. Like hunger and fear, it operates deep beneath the surface of your life. It's a barometer of something else. It's a gauge. That's why it's a little frightening to get a boner when you don't want one. It's a little disheartening, a little unusual, and a little scary. Also quite exciting. I can get one from a magazine. A good-looking car. A hot tub. A *real* man. (Just kidding.) I went skinny-dipping once in an ice-cold lake; got a chubby.

This makes activities like dancing difficult. During the slow numbers in high school I always wondered if a girl could tell if I liked her. They can tell, can't they? Well, can't they?

Guys can't tell about women, though. There's no visible sign. If we're skinny-dipping in that icy lake you can tell she's *cold*. Is that the same as excited? There ought to be a signal to let us know when we're making fools of ourselves.

Men usually don't make a big deal out of what they've got until women make it a big deal. Until sexual awareness hits, the penis is just something that performs a useful function. Then it suddenly develops a mind of its own. The point is that guys never really notice what's between their legs until they notice women. Then the *only* thing we relate it to is women.

Penis envy really only exists among guys.

I learned this when I was still just a little guy in transition from elementary school to being forced to shower with the boys in junior high gym class. That was a scary day, and sex wasn't even in the picture. There were several boys who refused to shower in public. It wasn't like they had anything to hide. They just did not want to be naked in front of guys like Tommy Rodriguez.

I say you've never seen envy until you've seen Tommy Rodriguez in the shower. Now *that* was envy. Seventh grade and he already looked like Burt Reynolds! (I really shouldn't compare the two since I think Tommy's been married to the same woman *since* seventh grade.) I'd seen my dad's, and even *he* didn't look like Tommy Rodriguez. I thought, something's really wrong here. I carried that frightening image with me for quite a while. Maybe because I kept trying to sneak glances at it. And that's not something you want to get caught at.

There's always a guy like Tommy Rodriguez wherever you turn. I've seen *Playgirl* magazine. *These* guys should be named Dick. If they got excited they'd probably faint from the blood loss. Even if the body could adjust, there'd still be some numbness in the shoulder.

But that's all behind me. Now that I'm a man, I'm finally comfortable with what I've got.

It's been over an hour by now.

Can we discuss, uh . . . testicles for a moment? I promise this will only take a few seconds because even the word scares men. We very rarely talk about it. Even God didn't want to think about it. He said, "We've got some extra elbow skin left over? Okay, use that." This aversion starts in Little League when you learn that you have to protect your valuable area with jockstraps and cups. That is the reason I've never understood why balls are spoken of in the same context as courage. If they were so brave, they'd say, "The hell with the cup!" Instead, they're the first things to shrink when you're really petrified.

I've also never understood why men grab themselves and say, "Right here! This is it, right here." You jump into a cold pond and they try to hide up inside you. These are not courageous organs. Courage is knowing when to get out of the water.

But wouldn't it be great if women's courage and nerve were connected to their ovaries? "Hey, right over here! Right here! Cook these. I've got your steak and potatoes right here!" Women patting their midsections, right where their ovaries are: "Yeah? Right here! I got your laundry right here! I work, too, you know."

Balls are one reason why guys have to be careful of hitting other guys. There's a certain age when all you do is hit other guys there. Even when you're little boys, you know that's where it hurts. You wrestle other kids and they always go for the nuts. I wrestle the kids on the set, and quicker than you can say "ooofff!" they go for the gusto.

This is nothing like goosing, of course. As a kid, you're always goosing other guys. I cracked my tooth in the bathtub once when my brother grabbed mine—and that was just four or five years ago.

The important thing is knowing when to stop goosing your friends. Usually it's when women start doing it.

Some guys never want to stop, though. They'd like to whack you—just *little* touches—only there's too big a stigma attached to touching another man there. You can smack it, but you can't make contact. The quicker the snap, the better, but you don't want to be lingering.

Once, camping in our backyard with my brother David and

Sam Hobson—one of David's older friends—we were, for some reason, all naked. It was innocent nakedness. I was maybe ten. This guy Sam Hobson had a boner. It was always a big deal to get one, although at the time you didn't know why you got one. He laid it on his sleeping bag and said, "I dare anybody to hit that," because he knew he was bigger than everybody else. I've always been proud of my brother David for what he did. Like a flash he was out of his sleeping bag, and he slapped it. Hard. So hard that I burst out laughing from fear. David, on the other hand, ran away as fast as he could. Naked. And Sam Hobson—also naked—ran after him.

Big Sam and the Twins.

Sadly, Sam ended up killing my brother.

When you're a man, the penis is a very difficult part of the body to ignore. It's easy to ignore your liver; it's easy to ignore your pancreas. They do their jobs quietly, and you really only know about them when they malfunction. The penis always lets you know it's there. It shifts, moves, rises and swells with the tides, gets caught in your underwear, too quick a zipper and watch out! It's got to be touched, positioned, adjusted, put in here, tucked over there, pulled out, put in—and don't forget to wash your hands.

It's always in use.

Some women say that's our problem; that we're obsessed with it. Then they say men's behavior—and even our cars—are an extension of our organ. They heap tons of blame on the poor thing. I resent that. What's an extension of the vagina—a purse? I once bought a red Corvette and my aunt kept on me about the extension thing. I said, "Yeah? Sounds all right to me. Who wouldn't want two tons of manhood?"

Believe it or not, I used to think women were just fooling around when they said all that negative stuff about men, and that they never really meant it. (They don't have what we've got, so what do they know about it? Figure out your ovaries and your periods instead.) Now I know that their antagonistic attitude is just a reaction to years and years and years of abuse from men and society about their whole deal. They've got a myriad of problems that we don't have. What we need to understand is that penis bashing has a lot to do with women wishing their lives were as simple as ours. Like a comic once said: "Women have babies, cramps, and menstrual cycles. We gotta shave? All right!"

All right? Clearly, they get the short end of the stick every time they turn around.

We should get over this. To me, the penis is very simple and not deserving of anyone's ire. It's not to blame. It didn't choose its shape. It's vulnerable sitting out there. It has the same problems as every other organ: it ages, it gets sick, it dies.

Uh oh.

Despite what I went through as a kid, it's my good fortune that my real name is Tim Dick. It forced me to focus on what's male about me. So much of my behavior and humor depend on those glandular feelings and associations. But only to a point. Women joke that men have two brains. Well, let me tell you: I control it; it does not control me. It has no life of its own. It needs me to live. I feed it. I take care of it. Without me it's nothing. It does exactly what I tell it to.

Unless I'm around women. Which reminds me of a story.

I once emceed for Sexy Flexy, one of the first male strippers.

There were eight hundred women at a club in the middle of Michigan to see Flexy and his greasy, pumped-up crew.

That was when I finally learned that women—especially in large groups of two or more—are not used to taking no for an answer. It was very illuminating. Maybe it's because they haven't been watching men strip forever, but they were rude and rude beyond rude. They'd grab these guys and the bodyguards would have to knock them off. Do that in a female strip club and they'll cut off your arm. Meanwhile, I'd be yelling into the microphone, "Hey, lady, that's not a roll of quarters you're reaching for!"

After four or five hours, these women got bored with Flexy's guys and they started pointing at me. I said, "Nah." They said, "Yeah." I said, "Nah." What they wanted involved dancing and looking foolish. Dancing is not a male thing. Dancing for most men is just killing time. "Can we go home now? Let's go, ah . . . make love, or something."

But these women wouldn't back down. So I started rolling my hips, kind of getting into it. (Hey, I was flattered!) Eventually I got $96 tucked into my pants. Then, suddenly, a group of ladies pulled me off the stage and ripped off my watch. They ripped down the entire front of my pants. They pulled my suit coat down behind my back, immobilizing my arms. I've seen the mob do this in movies. Then an older woman—close to my mom's age—started yelling: "I've got his quarters! I've got his quarters!"

"Ma'am, once again"—by now my voice was a high-pitched squeak—"these are *not* quarters you're grabbing." She paid no attention. Somehow I freed my arms and I elbowed this woman so hard that she crashed backward into a chair.

She had to let go. She fell down and crumpled in a heap. I didn't realize I'd hit her that hard. I was shocked. I felt miserable—until she somehow got back up, took a slug of some brown liquor, and said, "You're not getting rid of me that easy, sonny boy!"

These days women want what they want. And why not, especially if they'll take an elbow to the head and get right up again to get it. Women can complain all day long that men have all the power. I know a grandmother in Michigan who could show them a thing or two.

In fact, there are many dynamics in the world. But none is more important to me than the drive to procreate. Let me paraphrase Lynn Margulis and Dorion Sagan, from *Microcosmos*, their book about bacteria: There's no greater dynamism in life than life itself. The odds of life's existing are rare, but once it starts it's very difficult to stop. And we are part of that dynamic process of life: cells dividing and finding new ways to beat the odds. The whole universe, allegedly, is black and cold and nothing. Ninety-nine percent of the universe is an unknown quantity. And only a minute part of the one percent that's left is life. As far as we know, we're the only thing alive. There's no proof and no indication otherwise. Earth might contain the only life in creation. We might be far more important *and* far more of an experiment than we think.

Whatever the case, men and women fight and struggle way too much on their path to figuring out the truth. They are compelled to become unified and have a baby. Sorry, we weren't created to have sex just for a good time. The reason it's a good time is to get us to reproduce in spite of all the hassles encountered along the way. (Then we can have a good time, okay?) We just end up piling on all sorts of metaphysical attitudes and sociological theories, trying to explain why two species so unlike each other—and who often *so* dislike each other—absolutely have to get together. Ultimately, it's like eating; you can't help it. That's why the majority of the population is attracted to the opposite sex.

Some societies separate the men and women. The reason is that men get along better with men, and women get along better with women. But after being in prison, I know that we can't do that forever because it turns men—I can only speak for men—into very violent creatures. Without women around, we become very violent and very sad, and very uninspired and very one-sided.

It's called watching too much sports on TV.

My philosophy is that most of what I've done in life is because of women—and even more so because of my name. I got clued into the realities early. It's my half of the imperative of existence. I had to find a woman and reproduce. I'm not the only person ever to say this: Camille Paglia says this; Dr. Joyce Brothers says this; even Warren Beatty eventually *did* this.

As a kid, you can be so happy. Then you discover women and you're so unhappy. Then happy and unhappy and happy. These differences, this rhythm, underlies everything I ever wanted to say about being a man, and about being molded by my reflection in women's eyes.

As Tim Dick I just got to think about it more than most, because it all starts "down there."

Wow . . . I think I need a woman right now!

Honey? I have something to show you.

And get a couple bucks from the cookie jar. I feel like dancing.

animal boy

Little boys are animals. They're indestructible creatures made of sticks and stones and ball bearings. Their mission is clear: push the boundaries wherever possible. Keep in mind that teenage girls and raging hormones aren't yet in the picture.

Ah . . . ignorance is truly bliss.

I grew up on Marion Street in Denver, Colorado. I was born in 1953. Fascinating, isn't it? (Well, at my age it's important to test my memory whenever I can.) I hung out in this great neighborhood gang. Remember? You were in one. When our group of guys assembled, we were like little apes in a circle—minus the body hair. We had our own hierarchy, like in *Lord of the Flies*—only nicer. All the different personality types were there. It's funny how we still seem to be those same people as adults. Think about it.

In any group, a couple of kids always vie for leadership. One's bigger, the other smarter; both qualify. Barry Phillips and I both had leadership qualities, even though he was a year older.

In my big brother Steve's group, Barry's older brother, John, called the shots. I don't know if he was smarter, but he was a giant, so everyone was afraid of him—and that somehow made him *appear* smarter. John, and Barry's other big brother, Howard, liked to torture people. (At that age they called it teasing: "I was just teasing the cat/little brother/grandma.") As you may have guessed, the older Phillips boys are now in politics. Anyway, they used to beat up on Barry all the time. They called it "roughhousing," which is like men calling lying "bullshitting." Barry wasted no words. He called it "pain." Then Howard would point his finger at me and ask, "Hey, Dick, you want part of this, too?" And I'd say, "No, you big jerk, but maybe you'd like a Hertz donut."

Apparently Howard rarely heard my clever comebacks, partly owing to my mumbling them under my breath and running at full speed in the opposite direction. Or maybe the big fat idiot was just deaf. (Just kidding, Senator!)

When you grow up, size still matters among men, only now the size of your bank account determines who's the leader. It also helps if you're smart. And physical presence is still important. This means that a big, rich, smart guy is your worst nightmare. The big, rich, *stupid* guy, as a rule, inherits a car dealership. And, incidentally, if any guys from either of these categories are reading this book right now, please disregard the previous sentences. It's just a theory.

In the group there's also the kid who's so crazy he'll do anything. Steal candy? What brand? Drink sewer water? Gimme a glass. He lived outside the rules and you never knew what to expect. This kid was respected and feared.

Today, he's dead.

One kid's funny, another is good at sports, another rides his bike real well. And there's always the guy you can manipulate. That was Dennis. I was cruel to him then, but I'm nice to him now. Of all my friends, we're the ones who still stay in touch because, okay, controlling him is a thrill I just can't give up. All right, all right. He's used to it. His parents pushed him around his whole childhood, and now so does his wife.

And, of course, there's the kid you're always trying to ditch. It's an unwritten law of childhood that works all over the world. And the best part about it? The kid always comes back to the group. And you welcome him—so you can ditch him later.

Our basic transportation was the bicycle. Talk about a boundary stretcher. You could actually go places. Six blocks. *Sixteen* blocks! In any direction.

I liked meeting new kids, or going to the house of the weird boy from the strange part of town who wanted me to come over after school. I'd have to ride my bike. It was okay playing over there—but still sort of uncomfortable. What did "playing" mean, anyway? You just messed around in his room. Sat on his bed, then the end of his bed, under his bed, talking about nothing, playing with his stuff, realizing he didn't have very cool stuff—well, maybe a couple of cool things.

The worst thing was that strange people's houses always smelled weird. Right away I'd be thinking, "Wow, something died in here. It's that carpet. No, that old lamp. Both of them. No, it's that woman. Oh, she's his *mom*. No, his grandma. Her legs are weird. What a weird dog. What are they cooking? I want to go home. I don't like it here anymore."

So I'd get on my bike and leave. I'd be pedaling furiously until I'd cross a familiar street and, once back in safe territory, suddenly breathe easier. But I knew I'd crossed a boundary.

Bikes were also cool.

The rich kid always had the ultimate bike, right? When I was young it was a Stingray: banana seats and a sprocket the size of a quarter. You could do wheelies, but you didn't want to go long distances because the small sprocket meant you'd have to pedal like a little clown at a Shriners' convention. I asked my mom to buy me one. She wouldn't, so I made my own. Got a Stingray frame and handlebars, bought a banana seat. Really cool. Then I spray-painted it purple. That's when it stopped being cool. No way you could compete with a Schwinn paint job. They knew what they were doing.

Barry Phillips had a Bendix, with the two-speed rear axle. You'd push the pedals backward quickly to change gears, like you were using the brakes. What a marvelously simple piece of machinery. You really don't need fifteen speeds: "Oh gosh. There's a hill, lovey. I think it's an eight. No, a six." What is this—Tonya Harding's skating score?

Today, it's the same sort of overkill in cars. I have a car stereo that will leave messages. It's got a manual two inches thick. The manual that came with my wife is smaller.

One thing I don't understand about bikes is why boys' bikes have a bar between the seat and the handlebar, and girls' bikes have that V. Isn't it backward? You'd think the boys' would have no bar. If you fell off the pedals going over a bump, at least your balls wouldn't say an immediate hello to a piece of iron. (And I think we've all said hello to a piece of iron at one time or another, right?)

Of course, if a boy fell off a girls' bike and didn't have a bar to stop him—hmmmmm—I guess he'd drop down and have his balls mashed in the pedal crank and his face dragged on the sidewalk. Maybe the bar isn't such a bad idea after all.

Of course, if a girls' bike had a bar, she'd have to step over it and any healthy adolescent boy would probably give up a week's allowance to stand behind her waiting for a cheap buffalo shot. I know I'm right.

That explains bikes. But many boy-girl mysteries remain. Like boys' and girls' shirts. They button differently. What's that all about? Is it so you'll know when you're wearing a girl's clothing? "Well, will you look at that? I've put on my wife's blouse again." You'd think you'd know because of the floral print. But it's a fun look. Summery.

One thing you'll never hear boys—or for that matter, men—saying is, "Charlie, that's a good-looking shirt. Kind of a fun thing. And those trousers make your ass look nice. Can I borrow those?"

To young boys food is simply fuel. You run low on fuel and you don't run around very well. We'd get hungry about three-thirty every afternoon. Power-up time. We'd go right for the main energy source: sugar. Two big Cokes, Twisters, Twinkies, Hostess cupcakes. On school days we'd have a thirty-two-ounce RC Cola, a couple Pixie Stix, a Snickers, and some Wax Lips just to keep our mouths busy until we got home.

Sugar may seem like just sugar to an adult or the doctor, but I was much more sophisticated. I knew the value of consuming something from every major food group in the sugar category. Your sucrose, your fructose, your glucose. Processed sugar of any kind. Your cakes, gums, caffeine-based sugars. (Caffeine, as you know, runs through the entire chocolate family.)

There are, however, sugars you don't combine: Lik-M-Aid and root beer, Jujubes and Chunkies, Dots and Raisinets, Pez and Sugar Smacks. Chocolate milk is better with cakes, but if you're tough, you can down a Coke with a brownie. For a grown man, that's like scotch and peanuts. It goes, but not real well. Cake and beer is another one. That's why adults hate having birthday parties. Combining sugar-frosting roses with *vin rosé* is a lot worse than getting old.

My mom didn't like to cook, and my dad didn't barbecue. Good lyrics for a Johnny Cash tune, and true. But after my little brother died of starvation, my mom straightened up and began to cook for us. This noble attempt sadly resulted in three more of us dying. Kidding . . . I'm kidding.

When my mom *did* cook, she really went all out to please our palates. For instance, can someone please explain to me about stewed tomatoes? What are *they* all about?

And what's a cubed steak? Mom fixed it every Saturday night. "Oh, hey, it's Saturday night. Lucky us!" It was a gnarly piece of beef with a pattern on it, like it was beaten with a tire iron. Gotta love that gristle every other bite. Mom would lovingly accent the cubed steak with, you guessed it—stewed tomatoes. We called this gourmet delight bloody brains and shoe leather. "Oh please, Mom, can't I invite a school friend over for dinner?"

To be fair, Mom made great sloppy joes, but never often enough. We would have been happy eating hamburgers and hot dogs all our lives. But no. This is incontrovertible proof that there's something wrong with adults: they think you won't be happy having the same thing every night for dinner. Tell that to my daughter when she's debating between macaroni for dinner or macaroni for dinner.

My wife, by the way, is an excellent cook, but after years of marriage, my menu requests are seldom met. When we first dated, she'd actually *ask* me what I liked. Sound familiar? When you first date a woman, you get a lot of things that you'll never get again. She once made me twice-baked potatoes. I'd never had one. You take all the stuff out of the potato, cook it, and put it back in. I ate six of them. I said, "You keep cooking like this, I'll marry you." I married her. I haven't had one since.

As a kid you're dependent on a female, and that would be Mom. She cares for you, comforts you, and nurses you when you're hurt. Think about it, men. When *those* essentials are covered, you get to go out and play. Even today.

When you scraped your knee, Mom never panicked. *You* panicked—and loudly, as soon as you saw the iodine or Mercurochrome. "Hey, Mom, why not just pierce my chest with a kitchen knife?"

Then it was Band-Aid time. There were all shapes and sizes. There were big pads for the really cool injuries that usually had a neat story attached. There were the standard "flesh"-colored Band-Aids that ingeniously matched the skin color of nobody. By the way, weren't "flesh-colored" Band-Aids and "flesh-colored" crayons just a bit racist? And what the heck were those little round dot-shaped Band-Aids for? You certainly couldn't let your friends catch you wearing a Band-Aid dot! Very bad for the image. (Tip for later: Never cover a zit with a Band-Aid dot. Everyone knows what's going on.) And what about Band-Aid removal? What a drama. Although my sister believed in the very slow incremental method, I preferred the popular *one, two, three . . . RRRip* approach.

When you were sick, Mom was there. Sometimes she even believed you were sick. Who's to say if your stomach really hurt or not? I used to tell my mom I had a sore throat and she'd look inside and say, "Okay." I was amazed every time I got away with it. Now I realize, it *always* looked red. Throats *are* red. I've looked at my daughter's throat and said, "God, is that red."

Moms. They're so amazing. They're incredibly caring women who, despite the most torturous and agonizing pain of their lives forced us out through an opening of laughable proportions, then loved and nurtured our needy little selves through our adorable infancies, our less adorable teens, and into our know-it-all adulthoods. They helped us redefine our boundaries all the way.

On the other hand, what else did they have to do with their lives?

Once fueled up with sugar, our bikes parked nearby, we'd lie around on glorious summer days, blades of grass in our mouths, plotting what to do next. It was all very innocent, but the potential for trouble remained. We were tiny Neanderthals, after all. But unlike our sloped-forehead forefathers, we couldn't hunt for meat; we could only hunt up mischief. Then mischief was shooting out Mrs. Campbell's windows with a BB gun. Today I guess it would be shooting out her windows with an AK-47. This reminds me of hearing Bob Talbert, a Detroit *Free Press* feature writer, talking about the problems with kids twenty years ago—and today. Then: not dressing properly, not being quiet in the cafeteria, and not finishing meals. Now: pregnancy, gunfire, and barbiturates.

This is social progress?

I think what gets me the most, though, is that somehow kids today don't share our sense of childhood wonderment. When's the last time you heard "Ollie, Ollie, Oxen Free?" or seen the neighborhood kids play Kick the Can or Capture the Flag? Did we just drop the ball on this generation? Is it just not safe anymore? Are we not generous enough to teach this stuff to our kids?

When I was little I asked for a BB gun. My mom and dad looked at me like I was crazy. "Are you kidding?"

Did it sound like I was kidding? It was a Daisy handgun, very cool. "Can't you just give me the money?" I said.

Unfortunately, it cost $24 and they weren't about to just go out and buy it on my little whim. So I did the age-old kid thing and whined for a couple of hours. Finally, they said, "Wait until your birthday." Kids can't imagine a sentence more devastating than "Wait for your birthday." And I had nine months to wait.

Fortunately, that night, I found my salvation on the back cover of a Silver Surfer comic. It was an ad that said I could earn big prizes selling . . . seeds.

I sent for a box, and they actually fronted them to me. I mean, they *gave* me the product. That's when I learned that with trust comes pressure. I had to sell it, and pay them back later. To this day, I'm pretty sure I still owe them money. Now you know the real reason I changed my name: in case the seed people come to collect. They must be very old by now.

My family bought most of the seeds and ended up paying for the BB gun anyway. I still went door to door, which turned out to be good practice for later in life when I'd make a quick $300 as an independent salesman and then cruise for the rest of the summer. A bit of advice: selling Amway, mints, and magazine subscriptions was the worst. Seeds were okay.

Of course, I didn't tell my customers why I was selling seeds. "Hello, ma'am. I'm selling these wonderful seeds to get a BB gun, and then I'll be back to pelt your windows and annoy your pets."

Once I got the gun, I was unstoppable. Moving targets were an irresistible challenge. I shot a squirrel. Then a bird. After that, I stopped shooting anything alive. I liked them better when they were moving.

Instead I concentrated on harmless stuff like traffic lights, windows, cans, my little brothers, stuff like that. From a distance it doesn't look like you're doing any damage. Get closer and you can see the little pinholes where you've shot the glass out. I shot at our neighbor's window: "Ding, ding, ding." Finally, she told my mom, "Someone's been hitting the window," like it was the big Mystery of the Week. It was pretty obvious who did it. Before I shot it out, the window *was* across from my room.

Just last year I confessed to my mother that I shot out that window. She said, "No, you didn't."

"Yes, I did."

She got really mad at me. I tried to calm her, "Maybe I should just go back there and tell her I'll replace it or something."

"It's too late now," my mom said. "She's dead!"

"Oh. In that case there's no sense in me worrying about it."

My mom wanted to know why I'd do something like that. I said, "Mom, there's lots of things boys do that they're not sure why they do it." (Understand that and you'll understand men.)

Like shooting at my grandmother. She was old, and she never complained. I don't think she actually felt it. If we concentrated on one leg we could actually get her to wobble a little bit. We told her it was carpet mites biting the backs of her legs. BBs won't really puncture the skin, but they'll sure raise one beauty of a welt.

All right. I never really shot at my grandmother—as far as you know.

BB guns are fun, but, let's face it, not very loud and not very destructive. And if boys love anything, they love noisy explosions and creative demolition. Boys destroy because we're hostile. We're built hostile.

Blowing stuff up is a rite of boyhood that continues well into manhood. We're contractors *and* soldiers. You can't destroy stuff unless you build it first. We're very good at this: why else would the United States be the home of Caterpillar tractors *and* Seawolf subs.

This dynamic is very basic. What starts with sparklers and smoke bombs later becomes roaring car exhausts, motorcycle engines, rocket ships, and diesels.

It's all about combustion.

My grandmother used to help us get our firepower. Not that she knew, exactly. Awareness was never her strong suit. She'd take us to the corner of 54th and Federal, where they sold the stuff. To get in to the store, an adult had to sign a paper acknowledging to the salesman that she or he knew fireworks were being sold. We told her we were just getting sparklers. She'd sign, then wait in the car while we stocked a small arsenal.

Ka-boom!

Two M80s equaled a KKK. Four KKKs became a stick of dynamite. It could blow your arm off. We'd buy a gross. You'd fire one off, and it would make so much noise you'd have to save the rest for a year because you can't just keep setting them off without the police showing up.

Capsticks were our favorite. You'd strike them and they'd smoke. Four seconds after the smoke stopped there'd be a loud report. We'd sneak them into people's pockets. It would rip the pocket right out.

Ka-boom!

We were also into fire.

We burned everything.

We used to build model planes and set them on fire during mock battles. Nothing beats a burning model for realism on the field. The B-17 Flying Fortress bomber was the best because you could light every one of the four engines and you could actually see what it looked like going down. The black smoke. The smell of cooking styrene. Pure exhilaration.

One time I lit up the engines to provide air cover while my friend Chris was busy with the armored half-track on the ground. It was trouble. A whole glob of plastic fell off, right onto his hand. He started high-stepping around the alley, his knees almost hitting his chest. I'll bet he still has the scar.

This was dangerous stuff. Once I blew my thumbnail off trying to light a firecracker and throw it up so it exploded in midair. I was holding the firecracker while my brother lit it. Instead of lighting the fuse end, he lit it near the bottom. I couldn't even get it out of my hand. I'm lucky I still *have* my hand. When my dad saw what happened he just said, "You shouldn't hold them that long." At least that's all I could make out because my ears were ringing like I'd been to a week of Black Sabbath concerts.

But that was all he'd said. My dad was a man of few words. I liked that. He turned out to be extraordinarily cool where explosives were concerned. Once, he showed me and my friends how to make a mortar. From my adult perspective this seems like both a good and a bad thing. Dads are not supposed to teach their kids to be terrorists, but I guess he knew we'd try it on our own, so he figured we might as learn to do it the right way. I had to respect him for that.

One thing I always loved to blow up was the fish at Cherry Creek. In the spring the creek would fill with water and the fish were so hungry they'd eat anything. So . . . we'd wrap a cherry bomb in wet Kleenex, cover it with salmon eggs, light it, and toss it to a desperate fish. He would gulp it down and then blow himself right out of the water. The carcass would fly everywhere and then you'd have to find the head, and blow *that* up.

You should know that, as an adult, I have not continued to actively destroy things. The impulse is still there, but with age comes control and the threat of lawsuits. I've learned to channel that destructive energy into the positive belief that I, by virtue of being a man, can *fix* things.

If you believe the words "anyone can do it" or "as seen on TV" or "with just these few tools," chances are you're also heavily invested in mink-oil futures. I've made eight or nine trips to the hardware store just on *one* job.

Recently, I thought I needed to replace a ballcock in the toilet (someone had to be laughing when they named *that* part). It was running all the time. But after I replaced the ballcock, there was still a leak. Apparently, I hadn't properly sealed it. So I had to go back and get the sealer. Meanwhile, my wife was saying, "When are you going to fix this toilet?"

"I'm working on it."

"Pay a plumber. We can afford it."

Not me. I'm a man. But somehow, putting in the sealer, I twisted something too hard and broke the washer. They didn't sell what I needed, so I had to replace it in brass—which didn't seat correctly, and stripped the water tube. When I pulled that out it bent the tube coming out of the wall.

Now I *had* to call the plumber to put the tube back in the wall.

He said the reason the toilet was leaking in the first place was that the mount on the bottom was wrong. Did I mention that I had thought of that?

I ended up buying a new toilet.

That is when I discovered that some do-it-yourself projects should begin with the words "Yellow Pages."

We used to go to Crestmoor Swim Club and use the pool. My mother insisted on the half-hour rule: no swimming for a full thirty minutes after eating. Not twenty-five minutes, twenty-six, twenty-seven, twenty-eight, or twenty-nine. It had to be thirty. Otherwise you'd die.

I haven't passed this on to my kid, though. I'm a new scientist. I forcefeed her way too much, and then *make* her go swimming. Not five minutes or three or one minute after. Immediately after. I make sure she's still chewing when she hits the water! Of course, I'm with her when she swims. I watch her. I just don't believe this cramp thing really happens.

In fact, as far as I can tell, *no one* has *ever* locked up in the water and gone, "Oh, God. I should have waited two more minutes!" Even if the theory is true, and you get rigor mortis and sink to the bottom, isn't it conceivable that one of the seven thousand other people in the public pool will notice one kid in big trouble? Or will a sunbaked clan of righteous mothers rally at poolside, restrain the lifeguards, and say, "Let this one go down as an example to all the other wise-ass kids who don't listen to their mothers."

"Bobby, see little Timmy down there? On the bottom? Didn't wait that half an hour like his mother told him."

I wonder how long they'd let me stay down there? Would they leave the chalk outline underwater after I'd been removed to remind the other kids?

As we well know, little girls don't disobey their mothers. In fact, given half a chance, they'll parrot their mothers back to their brothers. "Mom said thirty minutes." They pick up that attitude real quick. And when they get older, they do whatever they want because they think that *their* rules don't apply to those who are already perfect. Meaning them. Rules are meant for guys.

Going to camp for the first time is like going to prison. I know. I've been both places.

The worst part of camp is being away from your parents and your normal life. Suddenly, you see yourself as a solo entity. There you are with a big trunk and a bedroll, some comics, and a picture of Mom and Dad, in a cell block—oops, cabin—called Potawatamie or some other Indian name. There are guys your age, an older guy who teases you, a straight-arrow counselor, and the camp director, whose mere presence and his habit of showing up unexpectedly makes your skin itch. You have to get to know the people around you right away and it's very uncomfortable. Because you're so scared you puke all over yourself and on the kid in the bunk next to you. Since you can't do laundry, your mom sends your underwear up in a box.

The same thing goes in prison. Again, you're alone for the first time. Really alone. Then there's the vomit stage. And the indoctrination period, which is the day most people get their impressions of who you are. If you're quick, you realize most other guys in indoctrination are going through the same thing. It's the guys who've been there awhile and know so much who are whistling and calling, "Hey, chicken, you're in *my* cell."

Now I'm sure the camp people aren't going to be too happy that I'm equating a childhood camp experience to the federal penitentiary, but the experiences were remarkably similar. Remember that rather odd guy in camp who stared at you, and then wanted you to be his close friend, to be his *special* friend. Years later he's the rather odd man in prison who stares at you, and then wants you to be his wife.

If camp was a scary experience, newspaper routes were a stupid experience. Nonetheless, every boy had one. I did. I hated it. You'd have to get up early, fold the papers, put rubberbands around them, and stick them into a heavy bag on a bike. Then you'd have to toss them on people's steps. Sometimes the rubber band would pop and the paper would butterfly. Then you'd have to pick it up. When it's all wet and you only have so many papers, then you've got to go back and get a new one for the guy.

I admit it: I wasn't a real businessman at that age. In fact, I probably have some apologies to make because I don't actually remember *quitting* the job. I think people just stopped getting their papers, and I moved on to selling seeds.

All the elements of boyhood come together when you're playing war.

War was big. Bigger than big. Girls never played, or if they did they just wanted to play at being nurses.

My four brothers and I—our whole life was based on warfare. We had an arsenal in the basement. We had toy soldiers. When we played with wooden blocks we made forts.

I think war—for boys and men—only exists because the toys are so much fun. Who wouldn't want to shoot a machine gun? Or go sixty miles an hour in a twelve-ton tank? Can you blame the Joint chiefs for buying weapons by the hundred gross, even if they don't work? You know those generals get films about new weapons that are real slick, then they sit in a dark screening room, chests heavy with badges and decorations, going, "Hey, neat!"

When we were kids, the Marx Toy Company (remember the Marx parrot, in the commercials? "By Marx!") made guns that were almost exact copies of the originals. Each year they would come out with a new gun that looked more and more like the real thing. No pink flowers or pictures of elephants, just camouflage-color direct copies of the ones Vic Morrow used on *Combat*.

Vic on *Combat* was like God in his Heaven. I lived that show and I wanted to be in that squad. So we put our own squads together to go against other groups. Our favorite expression was "Da-da-dow. You're dead!"

"No, you just winged me."

"No, you're dead."

"Do I look dead?"

"Just wait until I get over there. . . ."

We'd have arguments. We'd get so mad. It was great!

I requisitioned weapons purchases for the gang. "No, no, it's gotta be fifty caliber." Why? Bushes were "cover" and you couldn't shoot someone through a bush *even* if you could see them. But . . . but . . . fifty caliber could go *through* a bush. I told you it was great.

I think this memory is actually getting me aroused.

One kid we knew had built a pillbox in front of his house out of piano boxes. It was impregnable. So I took a Mattel bazooka, which actually fired hard little red plastic things that wouldn't hurt you, stuck a sparkler in the end of it, and shot it at the fort. It stuck in the side and set the pillbox on fire. They were stumbling to get out and I was the big hero because I had actually knocked out a pillbox. And nearly burned and shot four children in the process.

It was an accident, I swear.

I built a lot of model airplanes. I gained respect for the Faulkwolf. I loved it when the two sides would talk about their opponent's airplanes with respect; something about that still turns me on. "He was the best I ever fought against." It was like shaking hands after a hockey game or the Superbowl. It shows you're bigger than the conflict.

Conflict is something men must do, but you're bigger in the end. We've lost that sense of sportsmanship in battle, now. We've becomes dupes of ideology. No longer do the last two soldiers meet after the devastation and salute each other.

Today it's just called Miller Time.

It's amazing how fast childhood went. And yet every now and then I'll get a scent, an odor, a taste—and the feelings, emotions, sights, and sounds of childhood come rushing back.

Bob Hope once was asked this question: "If you didn't know how old you were, how old would you be?"

For me, the answer is thirteen. I'm frozen there. I may look like an adult, but inside there's a teenage boy just becoming aware, in charge of the equipment. While this may seem alarming, it's actually good news. See, there's a lunatic in me (and all us guys— call it the animal inside), who, unfettered, might do things like oh . . . murder, cheat on my wife, hurt my child, quit my job, drive into groups of people on the sidewalk. There's still a part of me that goes, "I can't believe this is happening. Cool. Neat. Wow." At my most basic level, I'm still that kid on the day I became aware that I was in charge. It happens differently for every kid. For me, my father's death on November 23, 1964, crystallized it. I realized there is no one here to protect us; that life can be taken from us at any time. Life is a great gift. God is to be both loved and tremendously feared. And the balance between the two is what it's all about.

It was a sunny November day. My father, mother, and brothers were driving home from a college football game when they were hit by a drunk driver. Where was I? Playing kick-the-can with a neighbor boy. For some reason, I had decided not to go to the game.

Mom and my brothers made it, but my dad didn't. I was eleven and a half.

This loss stretched every boundary I knew. I wasn't king of my universe anymore. In fact, I felt helpless, useless, pathetic. I had no control, and my scramble to regain some made me grow up very quickly.

Today, my dad's death reminds me of earthquakes; things that shake your foundation. I'll never forget January 17, 1994, in Southern California. With the first rumble and shake, a knife went in and touched my soul and scared me at a psychic level. Sometimes I hear a creak and I immediately expect the big slam. The pain of my dad's death was the same. All of a sudden my world changed overnight. One day he was there, and the next he was gone.

My mom was stronger than we could have expected. She

remarried—an old flame—and their love rescued us all. It took my brothers and sister and me awhile to finally recuperate. I don't think I took the time to grieve until much later in life, when I suddenly realized how much I missed the guy.

I would like to have known him now that I'm a man.

gilbert dennison's older brother's room

It was a cold, blustery fall day. Football practice was over and I was walking to my friend Gilbert Dennison's house. I was ten years old. The word was out that there was something there I *had* to see. Little did I know that it would change my life forever.

Gilbert and I tromped inside. There in the hallway was his dad's new gun rack. In the dining room, his mom's new china cabinet. Nice, but hardly the stuff to make young boys speak in excited whispers.

In his room, Gilbert opened the closet and pulled out a new model airplane kit. Surely this wasn't it. I had seen many P-51 Mustang kits in my day.

"So, uh, Gilbert . . ." I stammered. But Gilbert already knew what I wanted.

"It's in Bob's room," he said, nonchalantly, like this happened every day. Bob was Gilbert's older brother who had just gone away to college. "You can look for a sec," said Gilbert. "But if you hear my mom coming, get back in here quick."

I made a beeline for Bob's room, opened the door, and stepped inside. I saw it instantly. There it was. On the fiberboard wall, above the bed. In plain view. A Christmas picture. A Christmas picture?

Well, like no Christmas I had ever seen.

It was a *Playboy* centerfold of a young woman hanging mistletoe. And she had no top on!

Nothing could have prepared me for that sight.

Boom. Birth of a chubby. Unintentional. Uncontrollable. I didn't even know what a *Playboy* centerfold was. I didn't know what a *chubby* was. Had I understood the importance of that day, I would have taken a shower, put on a fresh shirt, and grabbed a couple of soda pops for the big event. I was experiencing my sexual awakening. Something inside me had stirred and come to life.

I mean, I'd seen my mom. But that was my *mom*.

Looking back, I'm amazed Gilbert's folks let that thing go up on the wall in the first place. Now I hate myself for not asking them if they were interested in taking in a foster child. In any case, I suppose I owe them and Bob and Gilbert a belated thanks.

My life has never been the same since.

I know what you're thinking: A picture of a naked woman changed his life? Exciting, sure. Important, maybe. But life-transforming? Come on.

You come on.

Let me describe it for you.

The young woman was arranging mistletoe. She had a Doris Day face and a Technicolor makeup job. She wore red high heels and really thick underpants that came up over her bellybutton. I call them "amples." (If there are briefs, there must be also be amples.) Her feet were spread in a very mannequinlike stance. Otherwise she was pretty naked. That is, she wasn't wearing many clothes. Like I said: She had no shirt! And there she was, smiling . . . at me.

Personally.

She seemed like a nice young woman. A typical girl next door. Three decades later, while browsing in a used-book store, I found her centerfold in an old issue of *Playboy*. Her name was Ellen Stratton and she was the December 1959 Playmate. Instantly I felt like I was back in Gilbert's brother's room.

"Hey, Ellen. Babe. How ya doin'? Let me get a good look at you. You know, it's amazing. You haven't aged a bit. Remember me? Little Timmy. I used to . . . no, *that* was Bob. Right, Timmy. A little older, but still crazy about you. I'm glad we finally get to talk."

In the foldout, Ellen was standing in a cheesy living room, the kind you see in *Mad Magazine* parodies of Madison Avenue ads of the fifties. There was even one of those big orange ski-lodge fireplaces. A real fashion statement. The whole thing brings back echoes of ascots and highballs and David Niven with slicked-back hair. I half expected to see men in double-breasted gabardine suits and women in slinky cocktail dresses in the background, drinking martinis, chatting with Hugh Hefner.

On the other hand, if I could have looked around the corner, into another room, I'd probably have seen her family—mom, dad, grandma, grandpa, brother Billy, sister Jane, and probably their dog—at the dining-room table, eager to devour their Christmas fixings.

"Ellen! Ellen, dear? Your dad's about to carve the turkey."

"Coming mother. I just have to fix the mistletoe."

(And she's doing it in her underwear, Mrs. Stratton.)

Or maybe Ellen was a young housewife, her husband waiting in the bedroom to tuck her in on Christmas Eve.

"Sweetie, Santa's almost here."

"Okay. I just have to let Tim see me naked for a few minutes more. You don't mind, do you?"

"No problem. Take your time."

What a guy!

Every time I went to Gilbert's house, I'd stare at that picture. I'd walk out of the room and just go right back in. I'd go downstairs into the kitchen, then make up some stupid excuse like I'd left something in my jacket upstairs. I was probably wearing my jacket when I said that. I told you, any excuse.

But I didn't want anybody looking at me looking at her. That was the first sign of hiding my face from God, as they say. I was embarrassed by the heat in my cheeks. Maybe I had a fever? All I knew was that I had to study the picture. I had to honor those stirrings. Hey, they were the first stirrings I'd had. I didn't quite know what was going on. I didn't know what to do about any of it, but I didn't want to take out any time to have anyone explain it right then, either. I just wanted more, because Ellen Stratton was the most wonderful thing I'd ever witnessed in my life.

This was the invention of the H-bomb. This was the discovery of electricity. This was the wheel and fire all rolled into two bosoms.

This was better than blowing up fish at Cherry Creek.

This woman had no top on!

In a way, the picture was both frightening and reassuring. I realized for the first time that, dumb as it sounds, *all women are naked under their clothes*.

Every women is naked under her clothes! Let me say that again: They're all naked! Of course, that discovery made me instantly distrust all women forever: they're hiding this! They have this power and I didn't even know it. It's just under their clothes! The girls my own age were not of the same species. This picture had nothing to do with them. Nor did I relate Ellen to the girls at school. I related her to the gym teacher, the French teacher, the cafeteria cashier—well, without the hairnet—any woman who was taller than me. It's funny how little boys turn into lecherous lunatics. They get the same glazed-over eyes as strip-bar patrons because they're undressing every woman they see. This was sex, not that I was clear about what sex was. I think I once got so excited about what I'd learned that I said to the girl next to me in class, "Can you imagine this sex stuff?"

Then I quickly realized, "Wait a minute! She's one of *them*!"

The girls I knew wanted Barbie-doll romance and valentines and "I think I love you's." The difference between them and Ellen was tremendous. Ellen represented a manly, sexual urge arising in me. I soon discovered it was a sleeping giant. A woman can be naked in *National Geographic*, but this woman was naked with something in mind. Her nakedness had a power to it, and therein lies the rub—no pun intended.

Of course, Ellen was so casual about decorating in the buff that she acted like she wasn't naked at all.

The husband: "Santa won't come down the chimney if you're still awake. Is Tim done staring yet?"

Or mom: "Ellen, grandma's starting to snore. Maybe we should start eating."

Ellen Stratton will forever be at that odd age that I was somehow never at. She's a young woman put in an older situation. I was always younger than the centerfolds; then older. I never had the feeling I could go out and find anyone my age who looked the way Ellen looked, and relate to her on a person-to-person level. She was always somehow apart from me.

In fact, her whole situation wasn't real. I know, because for much of my life I looked for a woman in that circumstance and found it did not exist. I never knew anyone who hung mistletoe in her underwear. I was never even in the next room while it was going on . . . to my knowledge.

I was always at the Christmas table, waiting to eat.

To be honest with you, looking back at how that day changed my life, I'm not sure why I didn't just take the picture off the wall and bring it home. After all, I couldn't stop thinking about it. Hell, I'm forty-one years old and I *still* think about it.

Ellen Stratton is probably sixty by now.

Ellen, wherever you are, you're always in my heart.

Sooner or later it's all about girls and sex. Boys learn about sex, and what girls looked like under their clothes, in many places. In my time it was from Raquel Welch, in *One Million Years B.C.*, standing defiant, wearing a skimpy item from the latest cavegirl collection. It was from the poster, actually; the movie was horrible. It was from

Ann-Margret shimmying alone onscreen in a tight blue dress, warbling "Bye, Bye, Birdie." It was from sneaking peeks at copies of *Argosy* and *Gent* magazines. It was from peeping through the bathroom window at the college coed my parents rented a room to one year. It was from whatever stories we could gather from guys who seemed to know what the unknowable was all about.

Even if they didn't know anything at all. A good line of bullshit goes a long way. Even today.

Once I woke up sexually, I looked at everything differently. It's a change of perspective. I even looked at comic books anew. Suddenly, I half understood what Archie wanted from Veronica. I'm still trying to figure out what Jughead wanted from Reggie.

I had a thing for Veronica. Betty was sexier, but Veronica had the bucks. Betty would have been a better wife, and more Archie's match, but he always liked Veronica's style. Both Betty and Veronica had great tits. I wish I could have told Archie about my great discovery: If you change their heads, it's the same body. Black hair with big tits, blond hair with big tits. Very attractive. Got a little chubby now thinking about Veronica.

Of course, James Bond was my idea of a man's man. I loved Q's gadgets, and the Aston Martin. Eventually I noticed the girls, and soon the worlds of technology and women merged. Bond's movies raised my desires to a fever pitch. Cleavage, strength, maleness, virility, and small shiny things that clicked and exploded. Those films were sex, so much sex that they were primeval. Ellen Stratton, the Playmate, was a woman alone. James Bond, however, showed me how to get the woman and what to do with her when I got her. God, was he smooth and stylish. It seemed pretty damn easy for him, unzipping the beautiful Russian spy's dress, her bounteous flesh spilling over. Or just happening to be on the beach, hiding behind a rock, when Ursula Andress came out of the water in that excuse for a bikini. Talk about lucky timing. For years I thought Bond's way with women was *the* way. This explains, of course, why I didn't date for quite a while. There was no way I could get girls into a car with a handgun. Come on. Do you know any women named Pussy Galore? My idea of a date was going to the hobby shop and getting a can of gold spray paint.

"Do you expect me to talk, Goldfinger? No, Mr. Bond, I expect you to die."

Bond flicks only came out once a year. *Argosy* and *Stag* magazines were always lying around, mostly at the barbershop. They were full of uncomfortable images like bosomy women draped over carcasses of dead sheep, or guys with guns and women with big breasts in ripped clothing. Your typical story was "I Ate a Bear After I Killed Him with My Bare Hands." Everybody in the illustration was angry: the guy was angry at her, she was angry at the guy, the bear was angry at both of them. Maybe the bear and the babe had a secret thing going on, and got surprised by the guy in the forest clearing—which explains why everyone was pissed.

These were men's stories, full of furious, unshaven studs with huge pectoral muscles. If a dick could be a man, that's what it would look like. You could smell the sex and sweat coming off the pages. Of course, I didn't know what these guys *did* with women. I thought they just rubbed chests.

Isn't that what "Argosy" means: rubbing chests?

I think these magazines were actually where Hugh Hefner got his idea for *Playboy*. He saw these illustrated macho rags and he thought, "Ya know, I bet men would like to see real naked *women* instead of bears. And pay for it."

After we'd overdosed on James Bond and other sources of sexual apocrypha, the boys in the clubhouse started coming up with some pretty weird ideas about what you do with girls once you "get them"—whatever "getting them" means.

You figure out that kissing is supposed to happen first. Kissing on the *lips*.

"Well, you kiss them. but not like you kiss your mom—like any of us still, uh . . . kiss our moms."

Even those of us who *did* said, "No, I don't kiss her. She takes a shot, but I . . . duck."

This is an honest but sorrowful indication of what men do. Our whole lives are about "getting them." And then ducking.

We used to go, "Girls, yuck." But once the stirrings hit, the transition for most of us was immediate. Some guys, of course, don't progress into this stage very quickly. There's always some kid with a weird name like Augie, going, "Come on guys, what are we talking about this for? Let's go make a fort!"

Even as adults some men would still rather hang out with other men and wonder what concentrating on women has to do with the realities of life, like business and war.

In the end, women are not much different from golf. With both, the mystery is never revealed. Right when you think you've got it, you suddenly feel like a beginner. However, the *illusion* that we can plumb the mystery of women remains.

Kissing, at the time, was pretty much sex as we knew it.

I practiced kissing my hand. Sometimes I could go for hours. I kissed it in bed. I used to imagine that I was a wounded soldier, and a beautiful nurse had come to see that I was all right. I was hurt, so she had no excuse to refuse the kiss. I guess this was a natural extension of playing war. Then, the point was to escape injury. It still was, but if by some chance you took a hit, at least the day wasn't a total loss. About this time I began being sorry the girls weren't interested in *Combat*.

I stopped kissing my hand when my brother caught me doing it. We shared a bedroom. Even at that age you had to have *some* humility.

I should make it clear right now that I did not then, nor did I ever, put my tongue in my hand. No, no, no. We had no idea that even happened. Imagine the horror at the idea of merely putting your mouth against some girl's mouth. And then some kid just back from vacation in Europe tells you that the French do it differently. You almost want to go back to playing war. "No way. Uh, uh. I'd rather be shot in the neck than stick my tongue in someone else's mouth."

Oh, how wrong you can be.

I wonder if it's the same for women? It must be. The only apparent difference was that they often practiced kissing with and on each other. (I didn't miss a thing on those sixth-grade field trips to the planetarium.) It's definitely something I would still pay to see. And why is that? Men liking women kissing women is so stupid. I don't think any woman fantasizes about two guys kissing. Once again, we're a very different species.

I don't think I'm wrong on this one.

Kissing your hand teaches you very quickly a most important lesson: the nose problem must be dealt with. It's unavoidable. You can't go right at the person you kiss. The standard kiss is direct. Straight on. No twisting. You pucker and squinch your face. Noses collide. It's inevitable. The only difference between kissing mom or grandma and a girl, is angling the nose. When you start thinking about nose placement, you know it's serious. Eventually, you figure out how to get your lips and a girl's lips together.

In fact, the whole sexual mess is about angles. You get way too much information as a kid. You figure out the kissing thing and then some older guy tells you where your penis goes during sex. What!?! When it takes this long to figure out the angles of kissing, you don't want to even bother visualizing how the rest of it works.

Not wanting to have actual sex at the time seemed a certainty, much like "I'll never eat broccoli." You should always be careful about saying "never." But at this point, confronted with all this information and, worse, misinformation, most guys just gave up. It was easier to blow up fish.

Not that we stopped obsessing about it day and night.

Some guys *did* forge ahead, and they were the lucky ones. All you had to do was get through that first kiss. And soon as the kiss can be performed with the slightest hint of confidence, you're saying, "Now what was that thing about the penis again?"

Spin the Bottle was the game that was supposed to teach us about kissing. Unfortunately, someone would always chicken out. We'd get to the precipice and someone wouldn't play. It's like welshing on a bet when you're playing poker. Suddenly the whole game is pointless. Any boy who ever experienced the disappointment of kiss welshing surely acquired immediate respect for the honorable tradition of paying off your bets. (Or is it because you know your legs will be broken?)

Spin the Bottle probably reminds guys of basements more than anything else. That's why guys still like them to this day. *Eating* in the basement is really something.

Once a young man gets the stirrings, and a little bit of knowledge, he's dangerous. He's on a quest to discover what to do with the hormone soup bubbling inside him. And just how does the young man harness this carnal lust for all things female, make her bend to his will, and let him have his. . . ? Hey, hey, hey! In typically male fashion, we're getting ahead of ourselves. No wonder women tell us to slow down.

For most guys there is one girl who will teach him a few of the basics. At this point, the basics don't amount to much: talking to the girl you like, then making physical contact through handholding and kissing. And most important, trying to disguise the awkwardness.

The most confusing part is figuring out which girl.

For most boys there are three types.

The first type *knows* something. She has something in her eyes, in her face, and you don't care or know what it is, only that you want her knowledge firsthand. That she makes the other girls mad only makes you like her more. When a guy makes other guys mad he's holding back something they want. This is the girl with a bit of experience who is also willing to keep going forward to get more. This is the one who wants to do things in the basement. She'll come over on Saturday to meet the folks and then play games with you, with the lights out. Eventually, she'll suffer the humiliation of seeing her name written on a wall with the word "slag" appended. It's the lunatic inside you that wants her. Not that she cares about you. She most likely has her eyes on an older guy; in order to know what to do with him, she practices on all her inexperienced volunteers. "Come over to my place because I want to touch that." Like panting dogs, they go.

The second girl you're in love with. She doesn't know about the yearnings, or at least she isn't telling. She delights in anniversary cards marking each week you've been together. It's okay to hold her hand. Maybe you even play war together. She makes a wonderfully chaste nurse. Unfortunately, this means you see her only when war breaks out. It's almost backward. This is what an old person's relationship is like.

The third type combines the first two. She actually becomes your girlfriend. For me, our first contact turned out to be a far more human experience than I ever imagined.

My first girlfriend was really sexy, but she wouldn't give it to me in the dark basement. I'd have to get it somehow; and I'd have to give something in return. An unspoken barter system existed—a good early lesson about women and relationships. We sat on the couch for hours. She, waiting for me to *do something*. Me, waiting for her first to say *yes*. But you see, I would have to *do something* first in order for her to respond. But I couldn't make my move until she said yes. The last thing I wanted to do was say, " Um, excuse me, but is it okay to kiss you now?" That's so uncool. So neither one of us knew what was going to happen. A few years later I heard that some older guy came along, dated her once, and "got" her. That's how it always was. Some other guy got what I wanted. Bastards. All of them.

Unfortunately, I never got to be the older guy with *any* girl. I guess it's too late now, unless I start hanging out at high schools, going, "Hey, want a ride in my convertible?" Not that I ever would.

My first girlfriend was, naturally, the first girl I ever kissed. We waited and waited for her parents to leave the house, or go to bed, or suffer heart attacks. Anything, just go already. When it finally happened, the kiss was warm and hot, but awkward and rushed. I'd never experienced anything like it before. It was nothing like my mother's kiss, thank god. Actually, it did remind me of my brother pinning me down on the ground so he could lick my face.

After it was over, I was pretty certain we didn't do it right. But we were both glad we'd taken the first step. One small step for Tim, one giant leap for his monster. Eventually it got better, and every time we got ready to part we knew the moment was coming, so our hearts would beat loudly, and I'd think to myself, "Wow, this is a wonderful thing."

Men look at women the way men look at cars. Everyone looks at Ferraris. Now and then we like a pickup truck, and we all end up with a station wagon: the best of both worlds. Women equate this with the lady in the parlor and the whore in the bedroom. Men are pretty functional, it's true. What's interesting is that we often find the right kind of woman immediately and then, because of a taste for the Ferrari and the pickup truck, avoid the station wagon for as long as we can hold out.

Excuse me while I duck.

Don't get me wrong. I know I'm objectifying women, but I do so without malice. I know in my own heart I don't mean anything bad by it. I just talk about everything that way. That's what all men do. We look at a picture in *Playboy* and say, "Whew. Nice lines." When we get to know the woman as a person, she's no longer an object.

I wonder if it's similar but reversed for women? Because of our appearance, they project all sorts of feelings onto us that aren't there: "That guy's like such and such, I can tell. He wants me." Then they get to know us and *we* wind up as objects. "I always knew he was a lug nut."

It's worth thinking about.

The danger is when men start out objectifying—with cars and toys—and then keep doing it. Women aren't like cars. Not remotely. We call cars and boats "she" but that's wishful thinking. Women are not objects. But that's the natural way we think: we merge, we fix, we construct objects. So the first thing we thought about women, after breaking that rock and grunting a couple times— "hhhrrgggh"—is "Here's a rock that moves" and "Whoa, boy, nothing else makes me feel like that except the Buick I've been working on." If we could have had sex with our cars and boats it would have been a lot easier. But we'd be a smaller species.

Young guys are pretty comfortable about admitting to each other the stirrings they've discovered. This is not something to be afraid of or embarrassed by. It's just the hormones taking over. Men acknowledge what's happened, and as with everything else in life, feel compelled to prove their prowess. In other words, they start making up stories about sex and how much they know and how much they've had. Some guys can bullshit right up to the limit. We're taught at an early age to do this. That's how you get status in the group, by passing off the biggest b.s. and not getting caught. Sometimes all the guys *know* it's garbage, and they still don't call the guy on it. What's the point? You don't get status that way unless you know something he doesn't—and then *you'd* have been talking about it.

The kid with the tallest tales was always the one who had just come back from summer vacation. There was no way we could disprove it. "It happened at camp. A girl who rode horses there did everyone!" We let him get away with it because we wanted to be part of whatever happened. I wonder what women said to each other: "You don't want to touch it. They smell bad." I want to know where they got *their* information.

One kid said his sister always had sex in the basement. More bullshit, we thought. But it ends up he was right. One day, we cracked the door open, looked down, and witnessed two people going at it. It was weird. It seemed like a traffic accident or something. We were mesmerized. We couldn't look away. Even if they had seen us, we couldn't have looked away. We knew what they were doing—but what in the hell *were* they doing? And on a school day?

Okay, so you're newly self-conscious and trying to figure out what will attract a girl. Cigarettes seem like a cool thing. But there's a difference you learn very quickly between what's cool to guys and what's cool to girls. And what's cool to one girl might not be cool to another. It starts out as a real crap shoot.

A girl I was in love with showed up once at the baseball field where I was smoking a cigarette with a group of guys. We smoked Kools because we were cool. I was excited to see her. The first thing she said was "I thought you were so nice, but here you are *smoking*." I'm thinking, man have I screwed up. Then I brilliantly countered by appearing aloof, since I didn't want any of my friends to know I'd just given her a valentine. Actually, I'd handed it to her mom, but only because she answered the door before I got a chance to run away. I was so in the habit of leaving things on doorsteps, ringing the doorbell, and running. You know, "Ding Dong and Ditch It." We'd leave sacks of flaming dogshit for some poor sap to stamp out. Naturally, she made it worse by saying, "I was just about to thank you for the valentine, and now you're smoking a stupid cigarette."

I promptly put it out. Come on—I had a crush on her.

As nervous as all this makes them, young boys still want girls to notice them. The problem is the way they do it. Girls want boys to say, "You look so pretty today." You—indirectly—want to say, "You have nice tits." Girls want you to say things that let them know you somehow value them and dig their looks. You want them to let you know that you're someone they want to sleep with. And nobody else. Ever. You want to know that you're turning them on with your boyish charm and your butch-waxed hair and your dad's cologne. Women want to know they're pretty, and valued, and feminine. All you want to know is "Will you touch my penis?."

I remember all the girls' saying things about Robert Redford, all of which began with "Oh, my god . . ." To this day I wish I would overhear someone saying that kind of stuff about me. "Tim makes me just want to . . ." "I'm so drawn to his . . ." "With Tim, it's like flying . . ."

I always heard stuff like "Gee, Tim, that shirt makes you look nice." And I'd think, "Yes, but does it make you want me?" Maybe that's what they were actually saying, but they weren't speaking in a language I could understand.

Nothing has changed. How else can you explain the store shelves full of books on how men and women can learn to communicate better? Someone should come out with a man—woman dictionary, like those English—French ones. Men say, "You have a nice set of tits." What we mean is, you have a nice package and you're pretty. We don't see only the breasts. Well, only for a moment or two. Women want to hear "You look beautiful." And certain men know how to do that. They learn the little trick. Anyone who wants to teach me can write in.

Bernie Broder taught me all about sex. He was an older guy who didn't bullshit. He felt compassion for younger kids because he had been there. He was a mentor. He bonded with us, and we weren't afraid to ask him questions.

So one day he took five of us down in my dad's fruit cellar and fondled us repeatedly. No, he took us down to the basement and we asked him point-blank: "How do you make love to a woman?" We weren't going to giggle and be silly; we wanted to know.

In sex-ed films, when you finally thought you might see something that would give you a clue to what was happening, they suddenly cut away to this outer-space-looking shot of sperm paddling furiously for the egg. What galaxy was this in? It was, now that I think about it, the classic comic misdirect. They got your attention and then went from pictures to the scientific data real quick because *they* didn't want to deal with it either. No one seemed to want to reveal what really went on.

We five listened while Bernie answered our question in his straightforward manner. "A guy lays on top of a girl and his penis goes in between her legs and into her vagina." Once again, it was too much information. The French-kissing thing and the tongue were enough. My mind was racing. Now how about a game of war? Anyone? Isn't it time to go outside and torture some ants with a magnifying glass?

"So, now wait, wait. You lay on her?"

"No, no, no," said Bernie. "You don't put your legs sideways."

I can't remember what we thought: rub up against women, kiss them. If we'd done it the way we imagined we'd get busted in fifty states today.

I eventually realized it didn't matter what I thought. When Mr. Happy decides it's time, he'll tell you. At this point Mr. Happy was so brutal an animal there was no way to communicate with him.

We later found out that Bernie was dating Ellen Stratton and eventually married her. Then they moved next door to Tommy Rodriguez and his family. Remember Tommy? This guy was in the eighth grade, had a family, and worked at a factory at night. Drove a car to school. I think the guy was forty; he just kept coming back to high school because he liked to shower.

I *knew* these people having sex were all related.

the eddie
haskell
syndrome

Guys never get girls when they need them. If they did, they wouldn't get into trouble.

Trouble for most young men springs from unfulfilled desires. Now you're on a roll. Testosterone is powering your system. You're all dressed up, but where's the party? You have no job, you have nothing to do, peer pressure is mounting, and you're *still* too young for the girls your age.

So you get into trouble. There are new limits to explore, but it's different from when you were smaller. Now you have real hostility, confusion, and insecurity. And mom can't fix it anymore. Your group of guys even starts falling apart. One friend is drinking too much and getting in trouble with his folks. The guy across the street can't hang with you anymore because he went off the deep end. This is when you start becoming a loner, and have problems respecting authority.

To deal with the stress, some of us developed split personalities: half model citizen, half hooligan.

In other words, we become Eddie Haskells.

I was an Eddie Haskell. With my friends' parents, I was the model kid they wished *their* kids would be. I made their brood look pitiful.

"Don't you look nice today, Mrs. Cleaver. That's an interesting tool, Mr. Cleaver."

I'd go on trips with these kids, and later their parents would write notes to my parents: "Dear Mrs. Dick, Tim is just a delight. He makes his bed and cleans up after himself. He's always welcome."

But when my friends' folks were away, I became Tim, the instigator, forcing these same kids to buy beer.

"Okay, Beav, they'll be back about ten o'clock. Now go get me a gun and some brown liquor and see if you find two loose women. Whatever those are."

There are lots of ways to get into trouble.

At school, we were forbidden to smoke in the boys' room. A rule that forbids is a rule that is broken. I would rather have smoked in the girls' room, anyway. (In retrospect, I would rather not have smoked at all. Smoking's not good for you. But then you all know that.)

We also had fights. Manuel Lopadeca was always in the "ring" with somebody. He'd get pissed at some poor guy and the word would spread around school. At three o'clock everything would shut down, and we'd all gather behind the gym. Eventually, Manuel and his latest victim would circle each other. *Smack!* A couple of blasts to the face, a little blood. It was a catharsis. Fighting was a way to rechannel unused sexual energy. At least it was physical contact. It was a better way to release aggression than today's knifings and drive-by shootings.

I only fought with my brothers, except for once, when I fought Bob Stirwood. He hit my brother, so I made him sit in an ant pile. That's creative retaliation. Then *his* brother came, and chased me up a tree.

These days, kids maim each other for scuffing their tennis shoes. Can't we go back to fist fighting when you only hit people you loved?

Sometimes our evil was premeditated.

One of my best friends kept maligning another kid in our science class about his, uh . . . unit. He'd say, "Jim Kerwin has a bald pin cock." He'd say it really loud and really often, because this kid was easily intimidated. And rightfully so. We'd seen him in the shower. Tommy Rodriguez's opposite number. He probably spent his spare time desperately scanning the hair-growth-tonic ads. Doesn't work. You really gotta wait out that transformation and not fear that it's already happened.

It wasn't Kerwin's fault he wasn't sprouting, but my friend Gus firmly decided that there needed to be a sign on a massive concrete pillar outside the science room, announcing Kerwin's predicament.

"It'll be more effective than me having to repeat it all the time," he said.

And he bet me twenty bucks I wouldn't do it.

"Not only will I put up a sign, I'll *paint* a sign," I said, unable to resist a dare. I went to the art-supply store, got a stencil and some black spray paint. That night, with adrenaline rushing, I fashioned a perfect rectangle on the pillar. Next I carefully stenciled, in metallic gold: JIM KERWIN HAS A BALD PIN COCK. It looked like a damn professional sign painter had done it.

Gus saw it and said, "You don't spell cock K-O-C-H." But he still handed me a twenty.

I started feeling really bad that I had ever done it, and was overcome with compassion. Not for stupid little Jim Kerwin and his peewee cock, but because I saw the school maintenance man out there the whole next day, scrubbing the pillar with borax—and wrecking some fine art work, I might add. I had always admired the guy because he took such pride in his job. Now I felt miserable that no matter how hard he scrubbed he wasn't ever going to get off that heavy enamel. I also realized that since I wasn't a born vandal perhaps I should consider a career in art.

Eventually they had to replace the whole school wing just to get rid of the monument to our ingenuity. To this day, we're the only ones who knew.

Actually, just me, now.

I had to kill Gus.

Among other things, trouble is a wonderful way to broaden your relationship with the police. That's right! In seven easy lessons, you too can be saying colorful phrases like:

"Damn, it's the police."

"Cup it, it's a cop."

"Quiet, it's the man."

And the bonus phrase if you order before midnight: "It wasn't me, officer. I was at my house, watching *Home Improvement*."

The worst thing about being bad is getting caught. This is because the excitement does not lie as much in the activity itself as in the thrill of getting away with it. Mischief is a game of cat and mouse. It's guerrilla tactics. This is not like playing Redcoats and Continental soldiers, where you line up in rows, advance into the opposing gunfire and keep falling over dead like good fellows.

Even as adults, not getting caught remains men's number one preoccupation. That's why men learn to lie—although we prefer to call it "bullshitting."

"Who left that on the sink?"

"I didn't."

But you and she are the only two in the house and she knows *she* didn't do it. She doesn't even have one of those.

"Who farted?"

Same situation. But somehow there's a smug satisfaction to not admitting it.

You're thinking, "She didn't catch me."

Oh, yeah? Think again.

Of course, what you don't admit to women is often something you'll go right up to a guy and do in his face.

Don't ask me why, but it's a sign of admiration. A symbol of friendship.

You can deny stuff to a guy, but he won't buy it. It takes one to know one. That's why we don't make a big deal about lying all the time with other guys. We're in the company of thieves. It's expected. Lie, lie, lie, lie, lie, lie, lie, lie.

Men even lie about lying. I'm a mathematical liar: you know, two lies make a truth. A guy lies twice in a row and he thinks that adds up to being honest.

These days I find myself lying for no reason at all. I lie to myself. This gets really scary.

I'm lying right now to you people and you don't even know it! Or do you? Tell me the truth.

There are lots of ways to get into trouble. To be forewarned is to be forearmed.

EGGING: Egg a car and you can put a big dent in the side. Let the egg sit there long enough and it wrecks the finish. That is, it never comes off. When you're a kid, there's always one Egging Night a year.

Fortunately, there was always some guy at the PTA meetings who said, "Oh, they're just kids. Give 'em a break." I think he owned the grocery store. "Oh, and tell your kids I've got pears that aren't moving, just rotting. Maybe they should do a fruit night."

"DAD, CAN I HAVE THE CAR KEYS?: I'm not talking about serious heisting here. Just kid stuff, like borrowing your parents' car without asking. Before you're sixteen. Now, I didn't do this, of course—to the best of their knowledge. Between you and me, I *did* take their car around the block once, and my heart beat so fast and so hard that I thought it would burst out of my chest and go right through the windshield. Suddenly, that's all I could think about. I started freaking out. If it came through my chest, I'd probably look down and try to stuff it back in or something. And while I was looking down, some neighbor lady walking her poodle would, at that very moment, decide to cross the street, and I'd look up—oh, my god—and with the skill of a race car driver, I'd swerve out of her way just in time, and plow right into a tree instead. I sped home in neutral and spent the rest of the day recovering.

One guy I knew actually took his parents' car to parties. We'd be out, drinking, flying around at ninety mph in his mom's Mercury Marquis station wagon. They'd be out to dinner, thinking it was in the garage. Just before they'd come home, we'd get back, shut the garage, rush inside. The car would still be going "tick, tick, tick, tick, sss, ssss," and there'd be six guys just sitting down in the living room as his parents walked in.

They'd say, "So, what have you guys been doing?"

"Oh, nothing."

"You mean you've been sitting here all night with your coats on?"

"It's cold."

DONUTS: When you're out in the folk's "borrowed" car, you can have lots of fun making donuts. Here's the recipe: You pull the car onto someone's freshly cut lawn, crank the steering wheel as far as it will go and then just floor it. You'll be making giant donuts in no time! The constant spinning action creates a lovely mixture of grass and dirt, with a haughty bouquet.

This drives the homeowner mad. So you wait until the poor guy has repaired the damage—and do it again.

Occasionally an irate homeowner will lay small tank traps—sharp, well-placed rocks—hoping you'll hit one as you spin around and puncture a tire. (Try explaining *that* to your parents!)

This doesn't really work because once a guy challenges your right to be bad you find a way to be worse.

What goes around comes around. I know. I'm a homeowner now.

SILVERWARE: Some guys really surprise you. I knew one who came to school with bags of silverware. Other people's silverware. In art class he'd fire up the smelter, toss in handfuls of heirlooms, and melt them down into ingots.

He'd tell the teacher he was sculpting.

What he meant was that he was sculpting his initials into the bars, which he'd then carry home to his clubhouse. (A six-bedroom, five-bath English Tudor.)

This guy's in big trouble today. He was already breaking into homes to get the silver—a bad sign, considering we were only in junior high school. But I liked his motivation. He'd caught on early that goal-setting was a key to a successful life—even if it was behind bars.

Iron bars.

Do girls get into trouble? I don't think so. I've asked around.

Girls are more likely to be doing useless things like studying. Or going to afterschool functions to develop their social skills! Skills that don't prepare them for important things, like toilet-papering houses. Now, where's that going to get them?

Sure, some girls were chasing after the bad guys, which is another good reason to make trouble: boys learn early that we can't get a girl without a car and/or a prison record. A good grade point average and a working knowledge of *King Lear* can't compete with riding a motorcycle. When a girl's parents said, "I don't like that Tim, he drives that *bike*," you knew you were in. But mostly, if girls were into mischief at all, they stuck to petty stuff:

Stealing cigarettes. Swiping lipstick and earrings from the five-and-dime. Ditching school to hang out with college boys, and smoking *their* cigarettes. Hemming their dresses really short, then hiding them in their purses so they could change into them at the school dance.

Here's the big one: Reading romance novels under the bedcovers at night.

Reading?

But reading what? *Nancy Drew Meets Bernie Broder?*

Here's the big difference between men and women at the age when everyone's looking for action.

Take two equally equipped '68 Roadrunners, with the 440 Magnum—ah, what the heck, go for the Hemi with the decor package—vinyl top, the rally wheels with the custom rims, and the air-grabber system. Put four girls in one, four guys in the other. You send them both out to get a six-pack of beer, and tell them to be back at midnight.

The girls will probably be back by eleven o'clock. One beer is half empty and warm, with lipstick on the rim. The car's cleaner than when you left it, it smells like a mix of Chanel No. 5 and gossip. Everyone's chatting happily and planning how to get together soon for dinner.

The guys—if they ever come back—one is missing, there's blood everywhere, no one's talking. The beer's gone, a second six-pack is also empty, some liquor bottles are in the backseat, there are spent shell casings on the floor, butt prints all over the windows, a tire is flat, one fender's all dented, the muffler's hanging off, and a big piece of animal is strapped on the hood.

Two different worlds.

Some kids cross the line and one day they get into too much trouble. You're in their car, they pull into the parking lot of a 7-Eleven, and you suddenly realize you're in the wrong car. They're bored and looking for trouble. If there are no women, at least there's got to be some action. And action is definitely not going to the mall and walking around. This situation can lead to wrong decisions.

Petty theft was not for me. I stopped hanging around with these guys and set my own goals.

Selling drugs.

I'm not trying to be funny. It's public record. Eventually it landed me in jail. No one likes to go to jail. Prison takes away your freedom in a way you can never imagine until you've spent time there. Anyone who says prison is great or they can do it—fine. So explain to me why, if you opened the door, everyone would walk away. Once you lose your freedom, you never want to lose it again. Prison was the worst and the best thing that ever happened to me. It taught me in no uncertain terms to be responsible for my own actions.

It's tough to be lighthearted about prison, even if like me you've made it through. Still, I feel a bit like Audie Murphy, back from the war, full of stories.

Even today it's a big shock to people that I spent any time behind bars. They say, "You're not that kind of guy."

Well, yes, I was that kind of guy. Half model citizen, half hooligan.

And where I was headed was full of Eddie Haskells, too.

Prison is filled with guys in whom their lunatic is free. The lunatic is finally where he wants to be. He's in a place where lunacy works. The more of a lunatic you are, the better you get along with the other lunatics. Prison is a wonderful place for the lunatic to be since it's the lunatic in you that gets you there.

The difference between the lunatic living in the outside world and killing time in prison is that inside the lunatic actually speaks. He goes, "I didn't do it." Or "if I had a chance to do it again I certainly wouldn't get caught." The lunatic is always in denial because he never admits the slightest responsibility.

"It was the other guy."

"If you'd trusted me to begin with, I would have shot them both, no reservations. Then I would have burnt down the bank."

One guy I met actually denied that he'd robbed the bank even though he was caught at the teller's window with a ski mask on and a shotgun in his hand. I said, "So why were you in the bank?"

"That part I don't know. I don't know why I walked in there."

"But you had a ski mask on!"

"It was cold!"

"You were holding a pump shotgun and wearing a ski mask; what did you think the response was going to be when you walked inside that bank?"

"Well, I didn't think they were all going to go nuts on me!"

Like I said, prison's a great place for the lunatic. As for me, let's be honest. I didn't do anything. I wasn't even there when the cops busted me. I was at my house, watching *Home Improvement*. I was framed! I didn't do it!

And I was among guys who actually believed me.

The only place better for lunatics is the Armed Forces, because guys (lunatics?) actually sign up for that. You have to go in and say, "Yes." Of course, in the military you can also get weekend passes and see a woman.

There are no women in a man's prison. That makes the biggest difference in the world. You just can't take women away from men. It's devastating. Nothing buffers this. There's a sadness inside those walls, in men's eyes, that's pathetic. The loneliness. The anger. It was incredible.

My sense of humor about jail began in the holding cell. It had to. It was the only way to survive.

After the six-hour interrogation by cops who've watched too many cop shows on TV, the holding cell is first a relief, then a painful experience. But as bad as it was, it was only a peek at what was coming.

There were ten guys in the cell. The toilet's in the middle of the room. I remember looking at the can, then at the ceiling, then at the can, then at all the guys in there with me. I wanted to walk out. Yeah.

It was a smelly room, really depressing. My only thought was that I would die from fecal poisoning. I knew I would not be able to use the can. I mean, you can't take a dump with ten other guys in the room watching you. Peeing, sure; but the other? No way. Fart noises and other private smells are things other guys shouldn't be a party to.

Finally, digestion being as it is, things must emerge. I ambled tentatively to the can. I turned away and started back to my seat, but knew it was no good. I was committed. I sat down and suddenly all the men began moving toward me. I panicked.

I didn't have to. This still blows my mind.

What they did was form a horseshoe around me with their backs in my direction. Because they're men, too. It was a big revelation. These aren't just losers like me, but they're *men*. They do this so you have some privacy and no one can see in from the outside.

Meanwhile, I was also looking at ten remarkably nice butts.

The worst part, however, is that for about six months after I got out of jail I couldn't take a dump unless there were ten other guys in the room.

The real penalty of jail, as I've said, is no women. With no place for the testosterone to go—and the painful memory of where it *could* go—the flare-ups get very violent. And the violence is very unlike life, because real life gets mitigated by touch and feelings. In prison the touching and feeling were not my sort of thing. There was a lot of it; a lot of sex between men. There was also something else. I remember a guy who put his hand on my shoulder during a conversation. He wasn't gay, but I leaned in toward him anyway just because having *somebody* touch you meant a lot.

You could say one wrong word to a guy and he'd want to kill you. Literally.

I once offended a guy without knowing it. We belonged to the Toastmasters Club. The idea was to teach prisoners how to speak and utilize their talents. This guy was outgoing president and I was incoming president. I might add, for you gentlemen still in the club, that I never received my president's pin. Can we take care of this please?

The outgoing president had knitted me a comforter to give to my wife for Christmas. Of course, this is now one of my wife's favorite stories: I got this comforter from a guy who could have been a murderer and rapist. It didn't matter that he stitched this over a year with his bare hands. And at the time, I thought it was such an exciting thing.

We had a roast at his retirement and I guess I *really* roasted him. Hours later, he came to my cell and said, "I'm not here because I'm a well-adjusted person. I'm a *maladjusted* man. In fact, I have one big problem: my really big inability to take criticism or be fucked with. You just fucked with me. And for that you're going to have to pay."

You could hear me gulp in the warden's office. In a split second, he got me up against a wall. I realized I was going to die—and then a bubble popped right above his head.

When you're really in trouble your face gets this very odd, contorted look—like when you react to a vomit burp. One of the most amusing things, when my brother was about to get hit by my dad or had done something really wrong, was this look. Once, climbing a mountain with my brother, I slipped and fell. And he let me slip. Later, dusting myself off, I said, "What was that all about?"

He was howling with laughter. "The look on your face as you were sliding off that rock killed me!"

So as I was about to get my butt kicked, my life snuffed, this bubble popped up with my brother's face in it. And I started laughing. Suddenly the guy stopped roughing me up and said, "What are you laughing at?"

I said, "My brother's head just popped in above your head because . . ." I tried to explain it to him. I couldn't stop laughing.

He said, "You're crazy. Getting your ass kicked and you're laughing about it?"

"No, no . . ." I still tried to explain, "No, no, go ahead and hit me. I didn't mean to be rude."

He let me go. It was fabulous.

One other story: An overmuscled tough guy also wanted to mess me up. Just because he could. Just because he was bored. But he never did because I knew that every time I started talking like Elmer Fudd he'd lose it.

"Yeah, it's pwetty cwose to cwosin' time."

It would devastate the guy.

You could kick butt anytime. But you don't get to laugh that much in prison. It proved very valuable to me.

I called my mom once because I got moved up from a cell block to my own cell. If your crime is not violent and you behave well, it's sort of a reward. I got it on Thanksgiving. I walked in and went,

"Wow!" My own room, my own toilet! And two storage lockers. It was still the size of a bathroom or a New York luxury apartment, but I was in heaven. The floor had its own phone, as well, so I called my mom.

I said, "Mom! Mom! Guess what?" She said, "What's wrong?" because I wasn't calling at my usual time. And even then no one really wanted to talk to me because my stories were so interesting: "Yeah, Johnny got knifed, I saw two guys in the yard get punched, and the food still stinks. Oh, and there's a wedding coming up."

So I said, "Guess what? I got my own cell!"

She goes, "What?"

"Got my own cell."

"Oh," she said. "I'm so proud."

Meanwhile, I realize she's thinking, "Is this a joke? Hold on. Everybody? It's Tim! Davy is in Europe, Geoff's just graduated from Michigan State, Dave's got a brand-new job with a construction company, and my brightest son . . . has just got his own cell! I'm just bursting with pride. Look, Tim: Don't call here anymore."

Prison food sucks. Big surprise. One reason is that they road-test food on you. Hormel had some sort of magic meat they wanted to supply to the Army, but they wanted to let us lucky prisoners try it first. It was some soy-based thing. I don't think the Army ever bought any, so they turned it either into cat food or a laundry product. To be honest, I liked it. Especially the heavy barbecue taste. I could have been eating erasers for all I knew.

Lots of guys are behind bars for crimes that the government wants to do something about, but can't figure out how.

For instance, are stiff sentences for cocaine and other drug use stemming the tide? Right. *Now* we have crack—as if coke wasn't bad enough. This is a menacing trend. This problem is vexing the population. What I've learned in my life is that the truism is often true: If first you don't succeed try try again. Try it from another angle. Right now, it's like we're running through the forest with our heads down and banging into a tree, and just backing up and running into the tree again like the *tree's* going to move. Look up, step around the tree, and continue on your way.

Now, I'm in no way advocating drug use, just the rethinking of policies that don't seem to be working. The English plan for making opiates legal and monitoring their use is a small step. I don't think that people are saying, "Well, since the government is providing it, I might as well become a heroin addict."

Here's my solution.

Put cocaine in a beverage the way they did when Coca-Cola was first invented. It's soluble in water. (What did *you* think Coca-Cola meant?!?) There would be very little left for street consumption, and we'd allow the farmers in Colombia to sell a product we want. We could buy Colombia's whole crop. We could control it, tax it, and—here's the elegant part—make it into an afterdinner liqueur with somewhat the same effects, but it's also *extremely fattening*. Very tasty but full of calories. And believe me people would not be willing to get fat over cocaine.

You'd know the coke abusers right away.

"Hey, Frank. Put on a little weight, there."

"Uh . . . yeah, and I didn't get much sleep, either."

People will do anything not to get fat.

Oh, and no Cocaine-Lite, either.

Behind bars, men always steal glances at other men's penises. No matter how hard they try not to. You get used to it.

In the prison shower it was quick, but definite. You try to act as if you're looking at the drain, but everyone knows better. What you discover is that there are some men who would make women terribly happy. Also, some terribly misshapen men. I think when I say "misshapen" you know what I'm talking about.

In camp, you don't want to stand too close to a naked man. In prison, you have to—like it or not. There are no private facilities, which bothers some guys more than others.

In fact, in prison they like naked men so much that every time you finish a visit with anyone from the outside you have to strip down for inspection before you go back inside.

Kinda makes you want to stay in your cell.

Admit it, you've been waiting for this.

One guy inside liked me a lot. He'd been convicted of killing two FBI agents. (Didn't do it, of course.) He took care of my clothes. Most of the gay men worked in the laundry. It's a job; they get to sit and gossip.

Even guys who weren't homosexual before will, after a while, try something. Prison and Hollywood are exactly the same thing.

One night this guy came on to me. He tried to convince me that he could satisfy me better than a woman could.

My eyebrows went up as I recoiled.

Then I thought, you know, he's probably got a point there. Who could satisfy a man better than another man? We know what we want. Men hugging men is great. I think we should kiss other men like the Italians. And I think the day is just around the corner when you can blow another man.

"Tony, sorry you lost your job, sit down, let me blow you."

"Hey, let go of my ears. Hell, I know what I'm doing!"

This is one of my favorite stories to tell onstage because you get everyone laughing and suddenly two guys who have been high-fiving each other will stop, and their expressions will say it all: "Hey! What are we laughing at? This is off-color."

But I told the guy in prison "No."

Guys end up in jail because they don't have goals. Or their goals are the wrong ones.

If life is, in fact, a river, then you have very few options, all of them very clear. You're in a canoe. You can try to paddle upstream and live in the past, looking backward. Then you're going to hit something, and you'll keep wondering why life keeps hitting you in the back. Or you can fight the current but face forward, and not get anywhere. Or you can casually go with the flow and think about pulling over to the side now and then to explore the land. Smell the roses. And some people want to go as fast as they possibly can, straight to hell.

I think I was backpaddling and the canoe flipped over. I had no idea about looking forward and setting a goal. Then I met a guy in prison, at one of these groups, who summed it up best. The greatest missile in the world is useless, he said, unless it's targeted. A torpedo is adrift unless it has someplace to go. An arrow is pointless unless it hits something.

So it's important for kids—for everyone, even if you fail at first—to target something and head in that direction.

With all your might.

In a way, I was luckier than most. While awaiting sentencing I decided to give stand-up comedy a shot. The judge had suggested I get my act together, and I took him seriously. It was better than sitting around wondering why I wasn't getting any job offers. I thought that at my sentencing hearing the judge would take my efforts into consideration. He didn't. But, as you know, being funny saved my life—on the inside, in *my* inside, and, as I was soon to discover, on the outside.

Plus I had a few uninterrupted years with no responsibilities, to work on my material. Nothing like a glass that's half full.

the wonderful world of guys

Coming from my perspective, I can now with some authority discuss the Wonderful World of Guys. Because I've been with men for a long time, I now have a clear appreciation of their strengths and their weaknesses. And their real motivations.

I. GUYS HANGING OUT WITH OLDER GUYS

Being with older guys is potentially hurtful because, when they get bored, you're it. They pick on the younger kids who decided to hang with them.

On the other hand, you learn things. "So *that's* how you open a beer bottle with your teeth." "Wow, cigarettes really burn your hands when you do that?"

Older guys are always a step ahead.

They can also run fast and ditch you quickly, leaving you alone in an odd and unsavory neighborhood with no protection.

When you're finally older, the line between you and guys still older becomes blurred. Now you can golf with your dad. Now you can both appreciate the lady bartender at the nineteenth tee. And you can also, finally, say to him: "Oh, so that's how you open a beer bottle with your teeth."

2. GUYS HANGING OUT WITH YOUNGER GUYS

This is when you're saying, "I don't want him with us." And "He'll eat ants if we ask him to. He'll just eat ants because we'll *make* him." You don't often want young kids around because they're stupid. Plus you gotta watch them. "Great . . . Now where'd Billy go?"

When you're a guy it's tough being the designated mom. And, of course, the suede pumps make it hard to balance.

3. GUYS WITH GIRLS

Gotta be careful here. When the girl is younger, you're almost thrust into a nurturing role. Nothing else goes on except deflecting the occasional crush.

With older girls—forget about it. There's something sexy about it even when you're my age. As we well know, my first love wasn't my age. She was hanging mistletoe.

Younger girls have to be home on time. Older girls have homes of their own. Younger girls shouldn't even be out of the house. I think my parents kept my younger sister indoors until she was eighteen—or was that the cat?

I don't even remember the young girls out on the block, just the older girls. We'd always line up and watch them jump on the trampoline. I'm still excited by jean cutoffs. And any woman who can do a somersault.

4. GUYS WITH OTHER GUY'S GIRLFRIENDS

Without even trying, other guys are nicer to your girlfriend than you are. Even if they're not really after her, she'll find it easy to lean on their shoulders, ask what they're thinking and how she can get her concerns through to you.

"Here, sit in my lap," the other guy will say. "Let's talk about it." Or "Wouldn't you be more comfortable lying down?"

The longer the other guy's known you, the more he knows about the weaknesses in your relationship. Then he just fills in: "Oh, he doesn't ever listen to you, does he? How's your job going?"

"He never compliments you, does he? I think you look great in that red dress."

It's a sleazy arrangement, but they're in a very good position, especially if you and your girlfriend fight a lot. Next thing you know, he'll be saying, "Whoa, I'd *never* say that."

If you think you can trust the other guy, you probably can't. If you think you *can't* trust him, you're probably right.

I've been accused of this, but I swear I've never done it.

There was a perfectly good reason why she was in her bra and me only wearing a cowboy hat. You people. Always so quick to jump!

5. GUYS WITH OTHER GUY'S PARENTS

Usually, every guy is a nice guy with other guys' parents. I mean you gotta know the folks pretty well before you start insulting them. It took me quite a few years, but pretty soon I was telling my friends' folks to go straight to hell.

I remember I once went to this guy's house. They had a bar in the days when a bar was the proud focal point of any home. This kid wore lime-green pants with little duck patterns. In other words, he was a bad caricature of his dad. He'd stand at the bar—just like his dad—and say, "Grab your weapons, pick your poison."

This is one thing you've got to be careful of. Hang out with other guys' parents long enough and you turn into them. Look for the signs. It happens to their children. It can happen to you.

Lots of times we never saw other guys' dads. They came in late; they didn't speak. We knew something was going on, but we didn't know what.

There were also the other guys' parents that *your* parents didn't like because you went away with them and their kids on weekends and your parents knew they were giving you liquor. These parents were a little too friendly with the kids. They'd take you up to the cabin. They didn't expect thank-you notes, and it never seemed like you were imposing. They didn't play parent with you. So you ended up liking them. Another example is the guy whose dad had the kickass stereo or cool car collection. Everybody liked him. It really screwed up your contempt for adults when you found that some other guy's father was actually a great guy.

Of course, this made your parents pale by comparison.

"Wow. Joey's house is so cool. He has a color TV. His mom lets us eat on TV trays."

That was a big deal in our house, to be able to eat on TV trays. However, there were six of us, and my parents correctly feared that we'd make a mess. A big mess.

6. GUYS AT WORK

Because we live in the modern age, women now have choices that are just killing them.

They can have a job, not have a job. They can be married or unmarried, married with children, unmarried with children, married with children and a job, unmarried with children and a job, unmarried with children no job, unmarried with children who themselves have jobs, have a job and an au pair who has children, marry the au pair, have the au pair have their children, etc.

Men, unfortunately, have the same choice we've always had: we can work or we can go to jail.

7. GUYS WITH THEIR IN-LAWS

In-laws are fake parents. The hardest thing is getting used to calling some strange woman and man Mom and Dad. You pretend to be comfortable with it, but you never are. They know it, but they pretend they don't.

So many games.

Okay, I do it, but in a faux way. I know they don't take it as seriously as when my wife goes, "Mom! Dad!" In fact, since they're my in-laws, I don't even have to talk with them. This is a parent to whom I can actually say, "No!" without getting grounded. As in:

"You put mint jelly on *what*? No way."

"Nope. Don't really like opera."

I've never stopped to wonder what it would have been like if my in-laws had been my real parents. They only had girls, and that just wouldn't do. Every once in a while I kid them about needing a boy around. They're so anti burping and farting and hawking. When my wife and I spend the night at their home, the same thing always happens. I get up in the morning and clear my throat, and heads pop out of doorways along the entire hall, as if I'd just strangled their dog. The last time I saw the dog *it was fine*. Matter of fact, it was morning and it had just popped its head out of the doorway and was staring at me as if I had just strangled the family.

8. GUYS AT PARTIES

This is where you see the little boy come out.

Guys can be uncomfortable around guys they don't know, and parties bring out this troublesome quality most. This is why men are more likely to get liquored-up in strange social situations. At every party you'll see a disheveled group, with crooked ties, swilling brown liquor in a corner, talking sports, bonding.

If you're a guy alone at a party, just wandering around can be dangerous. It's no problem for a woman to accidentally brush a guy's hand—or any woman's—but let a guy touch another guy by mistake and there needs to be an awful lot of explaining before anybody believes it's the truth. You're embarrassed for a day and a half. Better to just ignore it, go join the guys in the corner, and get liquored up. A guy touched me once at a party and ended up apologizing three or four times.

"I didn't mean to do that, you know."

"I didn't think so."

"I mean I *really* didn't. If I'd known your hand was there I wouldn't have put it there."

"I know."

"I mean I didn't mean to touch your hand."

Unfortunately, there's too much pushing and shoving, especially at the good parties, to avoid the occasional questionable contact.

So if you're working your way through a crowded party and you feel a hand on your ass, you'd better hope it's a woman.

9. GUYS WITH THEIR BEST FRIENDS

This is a truly remarkable thing about men. If a guy is your best friend, in a way he's exactly what you're looking for in a wife. He'd be the ideal woman.

Now don't get me wrong.

THE WONDERFUL WORLD OF GUYS

The desirable qualities are loyalty and longevity. My best friends, most of whom I've known since grade school, have elected to stick with me through successes and failures. It's the history that makes our relationships exciting. It's the same thing when you've been with a woman for a long time.

Best friendship can also be a confusing issue, because it complicates introductions.

"This is my best friend, John . . ." and then you say to yourself, "Well, not my *best* friend. Actually, that's Pete. But I haven't seen Pete . . ."

The best friend is the coolest guy you're with at that moment, okay? Your best friends are the guys who give you respect—which is what all men want.

But none of them can do what my wife does to me in the bathtub.

THINGS MEN NEVER WANT TO HEAR

No!

I'm afraid it's not the starter.

Is it in?

Gee, I've never seen one quite that misshapen.

Tim, the school called.

What's this letter from the IRS?

Another guy saying, "Where is this relationship going?"

I thought you had money.

I thought you were going to pay.

From your doctor: That had to hurt.

From the masseuse:

Whoops!

How long has *that* been there.

I meant *really* sleep together.

women are people, too

What do women want?

A good question when Sigmund Freud first posed it, a good question now, and probably a good question a thousand years from now when aliens have overrun the earth and *they're* trying to figure out the answer.

To discover what women want, we first need to thoroughly understand them. Comprehending women's habits, needs, desires, and the difference between a dress and a skirt is really the key to a man's peace of mind and better relations for all. Easy, right?

Here's what I know for sure: Women are not the opposite sex, they're a whole other species. And that's it. Short chapter. Goodnight, folks. Try the veal. I'm here all week.

Okay, let's not give up so easily.

Unfortunately, as you know from reading this far, women are

pretty much a mystery to me, which at least makes my obsession with them completely justifiable. Just the sight of a pretty woman makes me want to make dinner reservations. I may be a guy's guy, but I can't take a man on a date and get away with it. But because I often talk about women as if I know what I'm talking about, I'm occasionally asked by complete strangers what a man should look for in a gal.

The answer is easy: breath.

She should be alive. Right away you'll be ahead of the game, and once you've established the presence of her vital signs, you can take your time looking deeper into the abyss.

Trust me, it's an abyss.

But don't take too long. Women hate to be kept waiting.

Before you understand women other than your mom or sisters—and remember, to other guys they're women, too—you've got to meet them. If you're a guy on the go, the women you want to meet are usually the ones you want to date. Okay, have sex with. These are the hardest women to understand, and they don't try to make it any easier, even though they want to meet and understand you—well maybe not *you*, bonehead—as badly as you want to meet and understand them. Wouldn't it be great if you could just be honest with a woman you find attractive and say, "Hi. I'm Bob. You're very attractive. Want to go home and rut like weasels?"

Unfortunately, this approach hasn't worked in the general population since the late sixties. Also, your name has to be Bob.

You've got to look for a woman who wants to meet *you*. But

how will you know? The way to tell is to study your courting cues. These all-important signals are the only way you can ascertain if the woman you're slavering at wants you to come over and talk, or if she wants you to douse yourself with lighter fluid and strike a match. While she sips on chablis.

The first sign is usually eye contact. Make sure, however, that she isn't looking at the guy behind you. Make sure *you're* not looking at the guy behind you. Other signals are the hair toss, the lip lick, the earlobe pull, and the hand on your leg. If a strange but attractive woman suddenly starts undressing in front of you while licking her lips, tossing her hair, pulling her earlobe, and touching your leg, it's a pretty safe bet she's interested in you, or working her way through school.

These are *not* female courting cues: when she's sucking on her own elbow, scratching anyplace, or adjusting her underpants.

I learned almost everything I know about women by being friends with them. When I was younger, I also got their moms to like me, which didn't work out so well since none of the moms really turned me on. I also took feminist courses. I'd always stick up for a woman's point of view.

My wife once invited me, quite by accident, to hang out with her and her girlfriends one night when they all went out and got crazy. I guess I just looked forlorn at the prospect of another night of beer and TV sports. She said, "Tim, why don't you go with us?"

About four hours into dinner, the girls got comfortable with me around. They dropped their "he's a man" shield and realized I was just another person. Just like them, only with chest hair. I was actually interested in what they were saying. I wasn't trying to dominate the conversation like a man. I was also outnumbered—so I was very quiet. I said things like, "God, that's horrible," and "I understand how you feel," and "He's a putz. Dump him." I crossed my legs and kept my skirt tight around my knees. "Really? Interesting. I can't believe it. Well, why would he say that?" Once I started doing that honestly, they accepted me. I was part of the girls' group. I was giggling. When they went to the bathroom, I wanted to go with them.

Of course, the big question is did any of this (before marriage) help me "get some"?

Nope. Even though it's ultimately the best basis for a relationship, if you're willing to be a friend, it's always tough to convert the situation into something more romantic later.

"I don't want to ruin our friendship," a woman will say, meaning either she has never really found you attractive or that you never ignored her enough for her to build up such an intense insecurity over wondering why that she had to fall in love with you to find out. Along with "You're just like a brother to me," and "Gee, that's terribly misshapen," the friendship excuse is among the most painful sentences a man can hear.

You can respond: "We'll always be friends. Trust me." Then dive in for a kiss anyway. But she knows better. Once you're cast as a friend, women have many ways of making a guy feel like slime for even considering defiling that chaste closeness for a little sex. After all, compared to true and lasting friendship, what is sex?

It's what you're after, stupid.

Looking back at some of the women I was simply close friends with, I realize that those relationships probably brought out the best in me. I could be myself. I got in touch with my sensitive nature. I experienced sympathetic bloating. I also wish I'd taken a shot at changing things. I can't help it. I'm a guy.

Women really like it when you're a man, though. It's tough to have a woman go for you if you don't show some generalized masculine traits. Assertiveness, decision-making, protectiveness, nurturing. A man has to give a woman the impression that he might stand up for her and take care of her. "Might" is the operative word. Women are very big on the idea of hope. I actually stood in front of my wife during a bar fight once. I responded so quickly that I didn't even think about it first. Believe me. The surprise result was that I made her feel secure and important, which in turn made her want me. And her wanting me made me feel important and secure. It also made me want me. That's where it got a little confusing.

And now you're expecting me to tell you what women want? Haven't you been listening? I don't have the first clue.

Some women will try to adopt traits they think a guy will like. They'll learn to talk about football and cars, the best beef jerky, and patio barbecues. This works, because if she's persistent enough (and cute enough), the guys will accept her—which is good. Then they'll forget about her because she blends in so well—not so good. If a woman is really good at being a guy, then chances are they won't even notice her because real life is rarely like in the movies when the tomboy takes off her grease-stained mechanic's jumpsuit, lets down her hair, puts on a minidress and some provocative underwear from the Victoria's Secret catalog, and stuns the leader of the pack into settling down with her so that they can crush beer cans against their foreheads *together* until death do they part.

The guys will call girls like that Charlie or Sam or Mike.

I should have known that it was time for a new approach when the girls started calling me Tammy.

There is an upside, however, to being a gal pal. You can learn some of their secrets. As stupid as they may sound at the time, they hold the key to, well . . . something.

Here's a good one: Women are just looking for a guy who will be nice to them.

Wow! There's some information.

The thing is it's true. Knowledge like this can help lower a man's handicap. And we need all the edge we can get.

While we're trying so hard to understand women, it would help if they exerted a little effort on our behalf. This might come in handy when they need our undivided attention—which seems to be most of the time.

Women. Grab your pencils. This one's for you.

To get a man's attention, just stand in front of the TV and don't move. He'll talk to you. I promise. Once you're past the initial "What the hell are you doing?" or the more subtle "You make a better door than a window," he'll start to break down.

"C'mon, honey. Really, honey. Honey!" A real man will just sit there and wait for you to step aside. If you don't, eventually, he'll say, "What? All right, what? I'm sitting here, okay? Okay, I'm listening!"

You will no doubt increase your odds if you're showing some leg, and you'd better know the guy pretty well before you do this. Otherwise there are questions to answer first, like "Who the hell are you and how did you get into my house?" In this case, it's possible a handgun could come into play.

Another way to get his attention is to fool around with his stereo equipment. Or mess around with his car. Adjusting the timing chain is a good one. If he has a tool pegboard, remove one particular tool and hide it somewhere special. And believe me, within a day he'll notice that it's gone and come right to you. Do be prepared, though. He will be cranky.

More attention getters: scratch the paint on his car, throw out his favorite old sweatshirt, or punch him in the stomach when he's not looking. His expression alone will be priceless.

And when you finally get him to look you in the eye, you might even be able to get the guy to talk about his feelings.

"Honey, I'd feel really great if you'd move out of the way. I can't see the television."

Innocent flirting is a way of expressing desire without actually doing anything about it. As such, it is one of our most genteel sports, not to mention low in fat and easily digestible. I know this because when I was young I was a pretty accomplished flirt. I figured that flirting was about as far as I was going to get, anyway, since I had such a horrible complexion. Even if you're ugly, you can be a good flirt. And flirting is safe because it is impossible to pin down. It's noncommittal. No one can ever be positively sure it's taking place.

"I don't know. I think she was flirting. Yeah, that was definitely flirting. I mean, I *think* it was."

One thing to remember: There's a big difference between flirting and actually hitting on someone. Flirting is like dancing around the subject. Hitting is like stepping on its toes. In other words, you're hitting on a woman until she flirts back. Flirting has to go two ways. A woman has to realize what you're doing and give you the raised eyebrow and welcoming smile. To have successfully flirted means you haven't annoyed anybody.

One of my most memorable flirting experiences happened at a party. It was beautiful. She had on a headset from one of those kids' toys like *My First Sony.* I had one on, too. (No, I'm not explaining why.) I'd known her for a long time and, frankly, we'd never acted as if we'd found the other remotely attractive. But within the privacy of the headset, it was suddenly fun to toy with the untapped energy between us. Besides, she started it. She was doing a little dance an inch from my fingertips. And then she started saying very provocative stuff into the microphone, for my ears only. "Oh, I think you're cute." "That's a great shirt." "I wonder what you'd look like naked?"

Bingo!

If I'd gone, "Meet me outside and I'll show you," I'd have crossed the line. Instead, I suggested we could make out behind the heavy living-room drapes. No, no! Great flirtmeister that I am, I was embarrassed. But I loved it. I'd had the thrill without the consequences.

It was like Chinese food, but without MSG.

The opposite of being bold is being in love but saying nothing at all. This is not to be confused with being too cool for your own good.

Silence has its complications. When I was in college, all I did was daydream about women. I fell in love from a distance more times than I can remember. It's easy. Plus you can attach all sorts of personal qualities to the woman without ever being disappointed.

"She's got a brilliant future in high finance. She'll get a second degree in entertainment law. She says I'll never have to work. She's beautiful even in the morning. And she longs to obey my every command forever." Sounds like my kinda gal.

Then one day you bump into her at the cafeteria and she has a voice like that Cola-Nut guy, and the energy of Steven Wright. Kind of ruins everything.

It seemed at that point in my life everything I did was to get a woman's affection. I wanted to have more money so women would like me. I wanted to look better, so women would like me. I wanted a Labrador retriever because I knew one woman who liked Labradors. I took a class because I saw a beautiful coed sign up for it. I'm not a stalker, but I understand what it's like not to have time for myself because I'm so focused on a loved one—even though she's never heard of me. Okay, it's nothing like the mindset of a stalker, only the strategy.

I fell so hard for one woman in college that I decided to follow her home. Just to, uh . . . make sure what dorm she was in. All that year I watched her. I wandered by her building, just hoping to catch one look. I knew her class schedule. I knew where she worked. The whole time I followed her my body was filled with a wonderful anxiety. But it wasn't enough. I was also trying to figure out a way to casually meet her, which meant that eventually I would have to step in front of her and say hello.

The alternative was to be caught in her closet at night wearing a penguin suit, and to try to convince her that I was really one of her stuffed animals, and would she take me to bed because I had been in the closet a long, long time, and I was very lonely. That's always a hard one to sell, and, regardless of the outcome, you're still out the cash for the penguin suit.

As I look back, it was probably a good thing I always chickened out because I'd kept my obsession bottled up for so long that I would have blurted out everything I'd been thinking for a year, things a casual stranger shouldn't know.

"I love your car, your house, and, by the way, where did you get those crystal doves on your dressing table?"

Eventually you find a woman you want to date. Now comes the hard part. What's the proper attitude to take?

If what you're after is a woman's undivided attention, give her none. You can wait out any woman. Don't make any moves. Don't show your hand.

On the other hand, you can give a woman too much.

I once tried just laying my cards on the table. I went to a club, saw a woman, and walked right up and told her what I wanted. I'd been reading *The Hite Report* and was eager to test out all I'd learned. She was speechless, and I figured I'd blown my chance. But then she said, to my total surprise, "No one's ever come on to me like that. Let's go to my place."

We made love. We made love again. We ate Mexican-style TV dinners. We slept fitfully. Two nights later she took me to her parents' house for dinner. I should have seen the signs. Because of my audacious approach the poor woman thought I was hopelessly in love with her and ready to pop the question. I was scared to death. Her father was really, really big.

The only question I wanted to pop was "Is there a back door?"

When a guy thinks he's going to get lucky, euphoria sets in. Then he wants to stay at the party, get drunk with his buddies, and see who else falls prey to his immeasurable charm.

Unfortunately, being so self-centered and greedy often causes a guy to miss his opportunities. His intended gets drunk, too, and instead of going when the going is good, he waits too long and then her mood takes a turn.

This is more commonly known as a woman changing her mind.

How a woman changes her mind is very difficult to understand. All I know is that it happens at the speed of light, without warning, and that unlike men—who wouldn't have the nerve to try this unsupervised—women have an absolute right to change their minds. A man must respect it, no matter how swollen his glands have become.

"But, Sherry, baby, you said this is what you wanted."

"Well, that's not what I want now. That's what I wanted a little bit ago, but it's not what I want now."

It's all timing with a woman.

"But we already made an agreement. I'm already in lovemaking mode. I can't stop now. And you're obviously excited and . . ."

"No, I'm going home."

"You can't go home."

And now you're begging, which is so very attractive. Once you beg you've lost her respect, and you'll never get any. Once you're begging you're in puppy-dog mode, and the last thing you will get is the bone. That's why it's good if a girl has roommates. Better odds.

Some guys think they're getting lucky when a woman tells him she wants them to sleep together. Usually, when a woman is *this* straightforward, a distressing surprise is just around the corner.

"When I said I wanted us to sleep together, I meant *really sleep*."

Another sentence from hell.

I tried "just sleeping" with a woman once, but it didn't work. We did not sleep. She slept. I was awake. Staring at the ceiling. Counting the holes in the acoustic tile. After some heavy making out and what I thought was an ironclad agreement to have sex, I couldn't stop wondering what she suddenly meant by, "I think our friendship is worth too much for this."

This used to happen to me all the time. But I only said it to one woman, who, believe it or not, is still a friend of mine. We wanted to fool around, but I realized that the question wasn't whether or not

I wanted to sleep with her, but whether or not I wanted to wake up with her. I know this because she asked *me* the question. Women . . . what can I tell you? Difficult as it was, I told her the truth. Seeing her in the morning would have been uncomfortable. And I'd have had to kill her. Fingerprints, murder weapon, details, planning, decisions. Just not worth it.

Women are always asking men, "How do I look in this?"

Any answer will be the wrong answer, especially no answer. Silence is truly deadly. When you hear the question, it's already too late to run away. The guillotine has dropped, and your head is already in the basket.

I have a question: Do women really think men can say something they'll want to hear? Or is this question analogous to boys' pulling legs off spiders? That said, try to say something nice. Deep down, women will appreciate that you're at least paying attention.

Visual tip: Before answering, tilt your head slightly to one side, take a deep breath in through your nose, and as you let it out, let a sigh slowly transform into a warm smile. The results are amazing, and often overshadow any words you might mumble. Be sure to first practice this in the mirror. Avoid the classic quizzical dog-head tilt at all costs.

I once watched a relationship end because the guy didn't understand this. His girlfriend came out of the bedroom wearing an incredible red cashmere sweater. Her hair was magnificent. She was so lovely I almost fell down. They say women dress for themselves, but clearly she was trying to impress him. But this guy just looked at her and said, "You got any beer?"

The look on her face. Her spirits just plummeted. She didn't even ask how she looked.

"You look really great," I said, stepping up to the plate. Sensitive man that I am, I had spotted the problem immediately and wanted to cheer her up. My reward was a gorgeous smile, half a lip lick, and eyes that looked at me in a new way. Later, when she'd finally dumped her putz boyfriend, she asked me straight out if I wanted to sleep with her.

I declined. I wasn't going to fall for *that* routine.

Besides, do you realize how many holes are in an eleven-by-twelve acoustic-tile ceiling? Three million two hundred thousand six hundred and twenty-eight.

She insisted. I resisted. She demanded. I gave in.

Do you know there are really three million two hundred thousand six hundred and *twenty-nine* holes in an acoustic ceiling?

Sadly, I've probably ignored how my wife dresses a million times without thinking about it. So now I try to remember that when I'm thinking she's pretty I should *tell* her she's pretty. Guys, don't be lazy about that. If she looks wonderful right now, say, "You look wonderful right now." But be careful, because she's liable to say, "Right now? What the hell does that mean?"

Another rule to remember is never comment on a woman's rear end. Never. Never use the word "large" or "size" with "rear end." Never. Just avoid the area altogether. Trust me. What are you going to say?

"Your butt looks good in those pants."

"Why, is it tight?"

"Yeah."

"So it's big?"

"No, it's just I like the way it looks in those pants."

"Meaning you didn't like it yesterday because it was bigger in those other pants?"

Women *always* think their rear ends are too big. You can depend on that like you can depend on the morning chubby. There's nothing you can say about a woman's butt that doesn't make her suspicious. There are many theories why, but I'm certain it's because the derrière is a woman's weakest area. She can't powder it. She can't use concealer. It's actually too far away to reach. She can't really see it well, from any angle. It's something they can't control, and they like controlling everything that has anything to do with their appearance.

Men, on the other hand, don't care how their butts look, especially when they go outside in the morning to get the paper in their underwear.

Very few things bother men. Women who don't shave is one. It's too much of a stretch. The guy will start shaving his legs just because someone in the relationship has to be smooth. Women grabbing a guy's love handles is another. Women can be particularly cruel about that. Along with the degradation of a woman's manhandling your spare tire, there's actual pain associated with the pinch. Remarks about a man's skin are another. A girl I danced with once said, "God, your pores are so big!"

I didn't really need to hear that, now did I?

Mostly, women say stuff about washing and men's general state of filth. When's the last time you asked your wife or girlfriend, "Did you shower today?"

Give a woman half a chance and she can shatter a man's confidence in less time than it takes to make love to your wife. And it's always in the form of a question.

My wife does this to me all the time. We're getting dressed for a date and she says, "You're going out like *that?*"

"No, this is a pre-outfit. I just wore this to get to the outfit. What do *you* think I should wear?"

"How about the brown shirt with those pants I just bought you?"

"Yeah, that's what I planned to wear! I just wore this to get to that outfit."

Meanwhile, she's changed clothes five times.

She should understand.

I've been asked when lying to a woman is okay. All the time would be just fine. As long as you don't get caught. Just don't get caught.

Here's how you can tell when a woman is lying to you: When you so completely believe what she's saying that it doesn't even occur to you to question. That's when she's lying, but it's a catch-22. Let it go.

Also, don't believe her when she tells you that you look great in her red cashmere sweater.

To help understand a woman you need to be familiar with how her body functions. Her period is a perfect example of how completely different men and women are. And why we'll never really comprehend them.

The period arrives every month, and each time it's something new. Whatever's happening to their bodies has never happened before. It's relentless. It must be horrible. Of course, I can only judge by her period's effect on me. And they say men are self-centered.

It starts with, "Honey, I'm so bloated."

"Stuffed from eating?"

"It's not like that!"

I guess that if you're not a woman you just don't understand this bloat thing.

"So it's like you ate too much?"

"No! No! No! Look at my swollen joints. Do my ankles look like I ate too much?"

"Well, if you'd eaten a lot on a consistent basis for, say . . ."

"I'm bloated, you idiot, I'm bloated."

"Like you ate too much."

That did it. Trust me, the only guys who can actually catch flying plates haven't worked since Ed Sullivan went off the air.

As I said, women's difficulties are very frightening. This is probably why men invented the calendar: to keep track of women's lunacy. (Lunacy, from the word *luna,* or moon—moon, tides, menstrual cycles.)

Maybe a good way to understand each other is to turn the situation around and put men in women's bodies.

"George, do the rough framing on the house today. I'm flowing like a goddamn river. And my tits are killing me!"

"Why don't you try those lite pads from Miller. More bulk, less filling." "I don't know. Jesus, I feel so ugly. And these zits all around my mouth. Do I still look pretty to you, George?"

Professional sports would forever be altered. "You know, Vin, Tony's not playing very well today."

"Yeah . . . swing and a miss . . . the way he handles that bat, he looks a little swollen around the wrists . . . called strike three."

Why do women keep making the same mistakes in love? Maybe because they actually enjoy buying all those self-help books like *Women Who Love Other Women's Husbands Too Much*, and *Women Whose Husbands Don't Love Them Quite Like They Used To*, and *Women Who Don't Pay Attention to Their Husbands and Lose Out in Love Because They're Reading Too Many Books About Why They're Not Loved*.

Guys read, too. There has never been a cereal box that didn't fascinate me. And you can earn free gifts—even today.

Actually, women are just searching for something, like we all are. A favorite lipstick, a scribbled Post-it. They want some reason to make love besides hormonal determination. They want stability. They want Fabio (first mistake). They want Robert Redford and Paul Newman (mistakes two and three). They want Marky Mark (a mistake even if he is available). But women are just like guys. They pick out the male Ferrari, occasionally try a pickup truck, and eventually settle in with the family station wagon.

What makes it take so long is what makes it interesting.

I feel a whole lot better now about being a man.

To tell the truth I didn't want to hurt anybody.

I just wanted this other guy's girlfriend because at that point in my life I'd decided it was time to get serious. Casual sex had become meaningless, and I was tired of trying it again and again just to remind myself.

I wanted Eric's girlfriend so bad that I kind of broke them up. I did it for a good reason: He never paid any attention to her. I couldn't figure out why, because when I watched her looking at him, all I could think of was how I wished a woman would look at me like that.

Then we got together and our relationship was not what I had imagined at all. I realized why Eric didn't pay any attention to her: because she was just bothersome. All that staring can drive a guy nuts. I found out it wasn't even staring. She was bewildered. She was in a constant daze. I don't think she could even see me. It lasted about a year. See what happens when you set goals?

I didn't actually break up with her, though. I just made believe she was a newspaper route and disappeared.

Only once did my chicken method of ending a relationship cause me any regret.

I'd been seeing a woman for two years. Her dad was extremely wealthy and owned a national chain of tire stores. Carrie Ann was incredibly attractive and smart. Plus she was born the same day and year I was. For a narcissist, this is unbelievably good luck. It's like a court order from fate saying, "Have sex." It's like having sex with yourself only you're not alone, like usual.

The only problem was that we weren't merging like I'd hoped. We were both funny, and when we were both "on" it was annoying as hell. We both demanded so much attention. Neither one of us knew when to stop.

When it got too heavy I just left.

Carrie Ann called and kept calling for weeks. But I was sick. I just forgot that I even knew her. It was the only thing I could do, partly because I was so crazy about her. What was I going to say?

Finally, her mom called my mom. My mom always said the same thing when this happened, "I stay out of my son's relationships. I just can't get involved in it." The other mother said, "Well you've got to do something. She's not going to school and she's not eating. For god's sake, this is getting very serious." My mom promised to mention it to me.

All I could say was "Mmm?"

Eventually I gave up my childish ways after being dumped about twenty times myself, and I realized I was just afraid of closure. I had to learn about finishing the job. Women need it, and men have a tough time doing it. (Some women avoid endings, too, but they're usually Playmates dodging Julio Iglesias's phone calls.) Now I know to just end it. Say it. Do it. Be decisive. Women demand that of men, which is good. Stop this bullshitting around.

I ran into Carrie Ann years later, at a party. She was with her husband. He was a nice guy. They showed me pictures of their three kids. Later, when I was about to leave, he rushed over and said, "Look, would you come to our house tomorrow and tell my wife it's over? Because I think there's a part of her that's still pissed." It wasn't really convenient the next day, but I will do it. I will.

A guy knows he's in love when he wants to grow old with a woman. It's when he wants to stay with her in the morning. It's when he doesn't want to leave the house. He starts calling sex "making love," and afterward he wants a great big hug. He loses interest in his car for a couple days.

It's that simple, I swear it.
So he does what any decent guy would do.
He starts, however tentatively, to think about marriage.
And that's when it gets really scary.

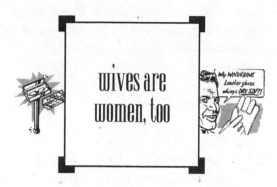

wives are women, too

The hardest thing about marriage is staying married. It's got nothing to do with sex. It has to do with money and power. Mostly power.

My mother-in-law made me get married. I'd been living with my wife for eight years and one night "mom" says, "I guess you guys are never gonna get married. I mean, you've been through jail together, you're living together, but . . . oh, forget it."

"Oh, well," I said, "put it like *that* and I'll marry your daughter tomorrow."

Actually, I don't know what we were waiting for, except that for a guy it's *never* the right time to get married. In this case, I think we were both stalling. I'm also a bit suspicious of any two people who don't struggle with that decision. For instance, I can't imagine meeting someone and getting married days later. I don't know how these movie stars do it! Marriage is a big decision. Big enough to procrastinate almost a decade.

Part of my problem was that I was still lusting in my heart after other ladies. But somehow I knew that I wasn't going to find another woman remotely as great as my soon-to-be wife. It's a good thing my mother-in-law finally spoke up.

I finally gathered my courage one day when we were having a picnic, and popped the question. I also gave my wife a big tourist pamphlet about Switzerland. I wasn't taking any chances.

She said no.

It killed me. I felt sick to my stomach. I lost my appetite. Our dog just stared at me, thinking, "If you're not going to eat your lunch, I will." Finally, I said, "But the Switzerland trip is yours if you marry me."

"Switzerland," she said, "is filled with precise, humorless people."

"Maybe I should have suggested Paris?"

For a minute it seemed as if my change in travel plans would rate a solid "maybe." But she said no again.

When we woke up the next morning, she told me that she'd slept on my proposal. "I guess I was a little rude to you last night," she explained. Meanwhile, I'm figuring I'm off the hook for this marriage thing for at least another eight years. I could afford to be generous.

"I asked, you said no. It's okay," I said. I might have looked a little too relieved because later that day she gave me a little box. Inside was a gold watch. On the back was inscribed: "Yes. I've reconsidered."

I liked the watch, so I did the right thing.

A lasting marriage is like a job. But here's the problem with jobs: They're great when you first get them. Then about a week into it you realize, "There are a few problems here." Then they get repetitious and boring. And pretty soon you think that the guy in the next cubicle has a much better job, which would suit you just fine.

The trick is to get past this.

The first time I dated my wife I envisioned us very old, sitting side by side on a couch. I've kept that picture in my mind forever. When you're old and ugly you're not really in the mood to go bar-hopping. The person you're with is about all you're going to get. Believe it or not, this can be a comforting image.

Sometimes the urge to merge with someone else really struggles to get the better of a guy. The urge is not unusual. It's not wrong. It's biology. The male drive to inseminate as many young and attractive females as possible before he passes out from skipping lunch is responsible for the rapid spread of our species and its survival. The trouble is that if you're married and you fool around, and your wife finds out, citing *Scientific American* works about as well as saying the guys in your bowling league all did it, too. Either way, you can end up sleeping in the front yard.

"But, honey, I did it for the sake of mankind."

"I got your mankind right here," she'll say, motioning at her ovaries.

A woman I once dated told me stuff I never wanted to know.

"It was just one football team and it was just one Sunday afternoon."

"Why did you tell me that?"

"I just feel better telling you," she said.

"Right. *You* feel better. You fool around, you live with it."

"But it's the seventies. We shouldn't have secrets from each other."

"I guess you're right. Here's a few secrets I've been meaning to tell you: I never liked *The Partridge Family*. I hate the cheesy powder-blue leisure suit you bought me. And, by the way, we're through!"

I think the lesson here is clear: Football isn't such a dumb game, after all.

I love spicy, rich food. I avoid it because it makes me feel both bloated and about to explode. Similarly, I don't believe that monogamy is a biological truth, particularly for men. But I still don't fool around because my wife would put a grenade in my pants. *That's* feeling bloated and about to explode.

I think about sex all the time. Still. That's the difficult thing about marriage. And that's why I love discouraging young people with a clear picture of marital reality: "If sex is the reason you're getting married, then you shouldn't be getting married. I wouldn't get married just to have sex with the same person forever. You get married to have a family."

Monogamy *is* possible. Painful, but possible. After a fast, torturous transition period, during which a guy has to sort out all these issues for himself, things get better and suddenly extramarital excursions are no longer an issue. This happens when we're about eighty. Earlier, if you count the side effects of the antidepressants or blood-pressure medicine. Either way, this stuff is tough for every man. The lunatic wants to stay loose. But by this age we know the lunatic well. It lives inside us night and day. The lunatic is tired of not having his way. The lunatic just wants to make trouble and noise. The lunatic wants to push us as close to death as possible, and pervert our last few drops of morality for its profane purposes. (Personal reminder: Call Stephen King.)

Now, quick! Get out your pencils and index cards. Here's my secret recipe for fidelity. First: I begin by telling myself I can do anything I want to do. That way, I don't act like a child and do something stupid just because I've been told "no." I don't curb my desire to murder people, either. I just don't do it. I add just a pinch of control, feel the feelings, let them simmer and evaporate. Never let your oven get too hot. Second: If and when sexual temptation is added to the mix, I can see clearly the right course of action without having my decision cluttered by my natural disrespect for authority. It helps if you season to taste with a woman who can accept that these feelings exist in a man, and if she can coexist with him and not make him feel bad about who he is. *Fini!* You can serve her that healthy, delicious relationship she thought only existed in cheap romance novels.

But be careful that she doesn't want you to wear blousy pirate shirts and change your name to Rafe.

Speaking of cheap romance, I always thought it would be great to live like an ancient Chinese warlord and have multiple wives. That would solve a lot of problems. If one makes you mad, you run to the other. On the other hand, what if you made them both mad? You're a warlord, for crying out loud. You run to another.

"Honey, I'm home from a hard day slaughtering barbarians."

"Don't talk to me, you armor-plated goon. Go back to your hordes."

"Fine. Be that way. I'll just go over to Gladys's or Helen's, then."

"Go ahead. You think we don't talk to each other during the day?"

Does sex change after marriage? I take that back. Isn't that the silliest question in the world? Of course it does. Only you don't want to tell your single friends the truth, because then no one would get hitched. And you don't want to think about it much either, because it's just too damn depressing.

The good thing is that reduced frequency just sort of creeps up on you, and stays with you, like midriff bulge. One day your pants are tight, but you know you don't have the time or energy to do anything about it. This is bad, but not as bad as one day realizing, *as you're doing it*, that two adults crawling all over each other and making funny noises are a ridiculous sight. Somehow you can't quite remember why this stuff ever seemed so damn important, why it drove you nuts and made you do crazy things just to quell that burning sensation.

Don't let this happen to you:

"What the hell are you *doing*?"

"Me? Look at *you*!"

I called a good friend of mine once to talk about this, because I was so worried about my libido's falling asleep. I didn't exactly know how to broach the subject. So I just blurted it out.

"When you're in bed, how much do you do it?"

He laughed. "Oh, I don't know. Last time must have been four months ago. Maybe five."

"What?"

"Tim, I have three kids, two jobs. You both want to, but the kid comes in, the kid's sick. Every time a Saturday night seems free, something else happens. And all these magazines say you've got to dedicate a night. Yeah, well, that's great; it's all good in theory. But if you're mad at your wife—and you're mad about, what, thirty percent of the time? or just irritated—then making love is the last thing in the world that you want to do. So there's a lot of things working against sex in marriage."

Suddenly I realized it was *marriage* working against sex.

Some wise guy with a small bank account once said that if you put a penny in a jar every time you make love the first year you're together, and take one out every time after that, no matter how much you have sex in subsequent years you'll never empty the jar. Maybe so. That is one reason why I used silver dollars. And when I took them out of the jar, I put them in another jar. I've got my golden years to think of.

Look, if we're hungry we eat. If we want to make love badly enough, we do it. But as life goes on and kids come and responsibilities grow, time becomes precious and there's not all that much room to fit in both lovemaking and a couple hours for the little lady to read *Cosmo*.

Sometimes a man has no control over himself.

My wife and I once walked into a real-estate office looking for a house in Los Angeles. Right away I sensed something. It came in below my defenses. I got a giraffe neck, twisted around, and saw a woman sitting in an agent's booth clear across the room. She did a hair toss and started rubbing her neck. Before I knew it, I postured: my chest went straight out, my shoulders straight back. We locked eyes. The chemistry was instantaneous.

Meanwhile, my wife was discussing second trust deeds with our agent, but I had a tough time paying attention. Every time I looked up, the woman was staring at me. She'd moved into the lip-licking phase. We were like two pacing animals. She could have been the mother of six, and I'd have still wanted her.

Finally, I turned to my wife and said, "Do you smell anything weird?"

She goes, "Why? Did you fart or something?"

"No. I smell something. Is there anything going on here that you can recognize?"

She looked around and said, "Other than that woman staring at you?" A smile played over her lips. "She wants you, Tim."

My chest inflated another millimeter and I said, "I know that."

"And you're telling her that you want her," she said, looking at my pathetic pecs.

"What? I didn't do anything!"

"Look at the way you're standing," she said. "You're posturing."

"Oh."

"Sit down."

"I just want to smell her, to be near her. It's nothing personal."

"Sit."

That's why I love my wife.

What happened had almost everything to do with smell. It's that pheromone thing, the little chemical agents we all give off that pretty much say, "Hey! You over there. If you like my aroma, I'm available." Or "Hmm. What's that cologne you're wearing?" It's always a good idea to have an agent do your negotiating for you.

"No cologne. But I didn't shower this morning."

Oh.

Dogs are really good at this. Fortunately, people are sufficiently evolved to restrain themselves from sniffing each other's behinds. But it's the same thing. It's out of control. It's animal. It's what that book *The Bridges of Madison County* is all about. It's why women swoon over big-screen male sex symbols like Robert Redford and Tom Cruise. Either that or the theater owners finally figured out a way to put pheromones in the popcorn butter flavoring.

When this happened to me at the real-estate office, my body wanted to find a way to stay there—alone. The evil lunatic inside said, "Take your wife home. Say you left your jacket behind—it worked at Gilbert Dennison's house, didn't it? Come back here and fulfill your biological destiny."

My mind was churning. I began to rationalize the emotional consequences. "I've *got* to see her. So . . . I'll kill my wife, quit my job, and take the real-estate lady and all my money and we'll go live in Indiana. I'll get a job in a hardware store and we'll just do it, do it, do it, all day and all night!"

I finally snapped out of it, but only because I heard my wife mumbling something about the thighs on the pool guy.

In school, if one girl was mad at her boyfriend, all the other girls were mad at theirs. Things haven't changed much.

Women's systems run better warmer. Men are like slow-pumping diesels and women are like high-test motors. They run better when they're hot. Men are more lopey, like Harleys. Women are like Ferraris. Those engines have to be heated up. I don't mean this sexually. I mean women seem to overheat a lot. They run better when they're angry. Anger does something to them.

This is not something you can avoid by deciding not to get the woman in your life angry. You have no choice and no control. She'll get angry all by herself, and if you just happen to be standing in the middle of her road, you get the full exhaust.

My wife can just stand there yelling at me, calling me names, for no apparent reason. When she finally sees how forlorn I am, and if I haven't apologized for anything out of abject fear or actual guilt, she'll say, "I'm not mad at you."

"Well, you're yelling at me."

Now she's mad at me. "Why do you always think it's about you?"

"Like I said, you're yelling at me."

"Why is it always you?" And now she's pissed off at me.

Women always think they're right. Women think men think *they're* always right. You hear this all the time. But women *really* think they're right. Oddly enough, women do have a calmness about them that suggests that they really do know something we don't. Men aren't a total loss, but women are completely confident in areas we're not, like the social graces. We just avoid all that stuff and concentrate on motors, bridge building, shoe shining, and knowing how to section half a grapefruit properly. Women act aloof from this typical male stuff because it frightens them.

And *then* they need a man around.

Honestly, I get angry always being in the wrong. Worse, I hate it when I realize that women have somehow convinced me of this. It's a very short and dangerous trip to the land of no self-esteem. Once upon a time a woman could have told me potatoes grow on trees and I would have believed her.

What is it with women trying to emasculate men? Is it all women, or just the ones I hang out with? It always starts with small things: how stupid I am, or demeaning my clothes.

"I can't believe you're going to wear that, I can't believe you're going to eat that, I can't believe you leave the seat up. You're so Cro-Magnon." It's always something *I've* done.

A woman will bitch and complain about having to do some

task, so I'll do it, and then she'll complain about how I did it or that I'm doing something for myself that has no relation to her.

These compulsions are really about a woman's desire to control something. Men, stereotypically, are the breadwinners, so women want to control the household. The cave. Naturally, we let them do it, but they know that if they're not bringing in the paycheck, they don't really control the household. I know. I know. Lots of women do bring in a paycheck. Must we lose everything?

We let them control the kids because, after all, they *have* them. We also know that if we just slip Junior a couple of bucks he'll do what Dad wants.

Women do control childbirth, which scares the hell out of men and makes us feel so worthless that it explains why we felt we had to otherwise own the world.

With men, being a bonehead is all related to our lack of concentration.

"Gosh, I just wasn't thinking. I totally forgot. I didn't mean to hurt you. That was *not* my intent."

"Well, what the hell was your intent?"

Every guy's been in this position, and you've just got to learn to ride it out. Sure, women expect us to think all of the time, but who can? It takes a lot of energy that would be better spent trying to find the Makita saw she took and somehow misplaced.

Still, men lapse in and out of consciousness all day long. Women are always conscious. They're always thinking. And as social, responsible beings, they think laterally: "This act would probably hurt that person."

Men think vertically. "What can I do to go higher, get there, move that, acquire this?" Men are on autopilot. We're always comparing ourselves to the next guy and what he's got. That's how we're defined. Within twenty minutes of meeting another guy, a guy will always hear, "So what do you do?"

Women ask the same question.

Actually, it's not such a stupid question coming from a woman these days. If a guy is an ax murderer, a woman should try to find out as soon as possible. If he's an emergency-room technician or if he handles dangerous radioactive chemicals, it's good to know right away. I know one woman who insists this line of questioning is a North American trait. In other localities, like India, it's "How many cows do you have?"

Here's what also gets under my skin. If men are such boneheads, what are women? It seems to me women get off the hook all the time. My wife's apologies are much quicker than mine. Maybe it's because she's so used to being right. I don't think men are wrong more than women. We just *take the blame* more than women.

Let me sum it up this way: When you're courting, there's a lot of good behavior on both sides—and you aren't ever going to see it again until one of your parents dies.

I've never gotten over being shocked that someone as physically small as my wife can make me so angry—and get me to believe it's all my fault. My wife is very much like the man. I'm very much like the woman. I'm the one who's always getting punished.

When we're driving, it's crazy. I'm behind the wheel and she's saying, "Turn left!" I'll turn left. Then she says, "No, this wasn't right." So I say, "Why did you tell me to turn left?" I could have driven this route seventeen times and she's going, "Don't . . . turn up here!" But I do, and then wonder why. Now I'm lost because I listened to her. Why? It's all about power.

"Why do I listen to you?"

"Well, I don't go *that* way," she says.

"Fine. But you're not driving," I say. "When you're driving I don't tell you which way to go. I assume you know—and very often you don't, and you'll blame me for not telling you where to go."

And at that point I'd like to tell her exactly where to go.

I have no idea why I listen to her when I already know where I'm going. If she had been driving and I'd done the same thing, she would have belted me. When she screws up, she just says, "Aw, well, this was stupid," and then just moves on.

I go, "Hey! Hey!" I wait for these moments. When she's finally wrong, I'm ready to bring up all the other times that she accused me of doing the same stupid thing and how I had to humiliate myself begging for her forgiveness.

But she won't cop to anything.

The only time I get an apology is when she's made the same type of mistake I have, close enough to when I did it, so there's no way she can say, with a straight face, that she doesn't remember.

I still felt I wasn't getting my share of apologies, so I got a computer just to keep track of this stuff. It's all cross-referenced, and I've even got it to print out pie charts of our transgressions as well as cross-referencing them to argument topics, argument duration, and intensity.

Take heart. Marriage can be fun. Wives are women, too. And they can be lots of fun. I love to travel with my wife. Her female sensibilities are so different that I always see the world in new ways. We're on a trip, we're highly excited, we behave better, the romantic spark that linked us returns, she reads the Autobahn and Autostrada road maps like a pro. (Besides, you can't make any quick left turns at two hundred kilometers an hour, with a big Benz on your tail.) We go to nice hotels, eat great meals, get dressed up, marvel at the wonders of the world. And the wonders of our enduring partnership. If you get away now and then, you can look at your life from a new point of view. It's refreshing. And I'm not just saying this to be nice.

If we hadn't had a child, we'd probably never come home.

Pretty soon we can take her with us.

As I'm sure you realize, I've been speaking in generalizations for comic effect. And I've changed some names to protect the guilty. As Kurt Vonnegut once said in the epigraph of an early novel, the innocent don't need his protection because "God Almighty protects the innocent as a matter of Heavenly routine."

In this book, I've said, "Men are like this, and women are like that." But not necessarily. I know many women who are like this. I try to stay away from the guys who are like that. That is not what this book's about.

The older you get, the more you realize there are fewer absolutes in the world and more perspectives. Stereotypes *do* describe the more common occurrences, but not always.

Life before marriage is a great time of life. Then one day everyone has to join the real world: jobs, love, and settling down. And no more bullshit. The people I knew who didn't settle down are now dead.

"Whatever happened to Joey?"

"Died."

"Marjorie?"

"Went to a commune and died."

Just want to see if you're paying attention.

Imminent death notwithstanding, this doesn't mean you have to sacrifice your ideals. It just means forcing your ideas to mesh with the real world. Once upon a time I thought I could change the world. Now, although I have influenced part of the world we live in, I still come home from work and hope that dinner's on the table. Before the meal, I'll watch TV and gather myself. This is something men do, like the caveman who just stared at the fire after a long day's hunting. We commune long and hard with the electronic embers, not wanting to speak with anybody.

Later, after I've talked to the wife and played with the kid, and helped clean up the dishes, I'll disappear into my garage workshop, where I can manipulate my own little world to my heart's content. And in there it's so nice being married.

men's zones

Men's zones are where men can be men, alone or among other men. They are the last bastions of the industrious male. Want to find a guy? Look in the garage, in his workshop, in the basement at Sears, at a strip club, at a drag strip, in the barbershop, at a men's club, in an M1 tank, on the deck of the USS *Missouri,* at a Greco-Roman wrestling tourney (well, maybe not)—and even in the bathroom just down the hall.

In each place a man can celebrate being a man quietly, without fanfare, without having to put on a silly party hat. Nor will he later have to justify to his wife the time he spent there. Women don't really mind our excursions into the men's zone. When we're in a guy state of mind, women would just as soon we do it someplace they haven't just mopped or vacuumed.

However, men's zones occasionally mystify women. "I just can't imagine what you *do* in that garage all morning."

Trying to cut and match corners of baseboard molding with a handheld jigsaw while dreaming of a miter box all your own. Changing the transmission fluid. Listening to the ball game on the old AM radio and detailing the tractor mower.

A man might just as well say he was meditating, only no man would cop to that, even if he knew the Maharishi personally.

"Ah . . . nothing."

Women aren't excluded from men's zones. The occasional "pop in" is allowed. But most prefer to avoid these areas unless they have no choice. Showing up unannounced in the men's locker room can cause major discomfort, both to the woman and to the naked man. Men's zone decor also leaves much to be desired. It's too dirty, too loud, too smelly, and the lighting is never right. How much fun can a woman really have in a room filled with war memorabilia, old *Playboy* calendars, and whatever neon beer signs her husband scrounged?

Men's zones are gun shops but not liquor stores, rec rooms but not gyms. Gyms used to be men's zones, but now there are probably more women than men shaping and toning. I've seen women in gyms who must be working out somewhere else just to look good enough to come to the gym. Boxing gyms are still pretty much a man's domain, but now some women are stepping into the ring and onto the canvas. I don't get it. Doesn't it hurt? Damn straight it hurts. It's a man's place to pretend something doesn't hurt.

Like many other formerly all-male provinces, the gym has become bizonal. Bizonality is burgeoning like the wild hair on a forty-year-old man's ears. Nothing you can do about it except trim regularly. For instance, boardrooms used to be male-dominated. Not so now. But this sort of social progress is absolutely the right thing. Besides, men have always conducted the *real* business of company and state in the executive washroom. Sorry, we don't have an extra key at the moment.

And what's this with women getting *tattoos,* for god sakes!

The next time I see Cher I'm going to have to have a word with her.

Like it or not, the bedroom is a woman's zone. I'd like to pretend otherwise, but between the color-coordinated bedspread and curtains and towel sets in the master bath, I've accepted reality. Men can brag about what they do in the bedroom all they want— most of it's bullshit—but she who chooses the petunia-patterned sheets is really running the show. I like to counter her bedroom victory with the furnace–water-heater room, definitely a man's zone.

The shop is still where the handyman lives. And every woman likes a handyman, although most don't realize it. You don't see "handy" high on those women's-magazine lists of qualities gals want in a male. (Sense of humor is always tops. Naturally I'd like to believe that, but I don't think Warren Beatty is all that funny—and look how he did.) Women just *assume* men are handy. And it's a good thing we are. Men make it their business to know how things work.

Even if a man isn't particularly adept, he will instinctively opt for deception over admission. This behavior, found in all male primates, is commonly referred to as "faking it." (FYI: In my recent studies at Cornell on primate behavior, I discovered that of all simians only the male Rhesus monkey buckles under pressure. In testing, nine out of ten readily admitted that they didn't know how to install a ceiling fan and ten out of ten pulled over and asked for directions.)

Men, on the other hand, get infuriated when a little drip stops the whole show. The mental stimulation of trying to figure out how we're going to keep from looking stupid after we've stripped a Phillips-head screw is indescribable. Besides, men rarely get an attitude when asked to take a look under the sink or at a carburetor, or to change a light bulb. When's the last time you heard a guy say, "Yeah, I can do it, but I'm just not going to."

That's only something you hear from your girlfriend, after she becomes your wife.

Sometimes, without any prior warning, you stumble upon the perfect men's zone. I knew a guy in Indiana who had a split-level home he'd designed himself. Somehow, he managed to combine his garage, basement, workshop, and den into one huge men's zone. You could drive the car into the garage, move a wall, and there was his workshop, den, and basement. The feeling is akin to being inside a church, especially if it's got a floor drain.

He had a floor drain. Every guy wants a floor drain. Who cares where it goes? Even if it's fake. A drain with a little grate on it means cleaning up is a snap. You hose the place down, and *voilà*! It's the kind of accessory that can make a guy speak French against his will.

Let me take you on a tour.

Along one wall was a very cool particle-board work area. He didn't have to worry about damaging it because it was built to be damaged. A woman would want the surface varnished and you wouldn't be able to put anything on it without a coaster. They'd want it pretty-looking to begin with. This bench looked crappy when it was installed. Perfect.

All the machines that powered the house were also in his area. But they were cleaned up and polished as though on display. This guy didn't *hide* the furnace. It was spit-shined and ready to be presented. The water heater was immaculate and without rust. Women generally want these things out of sight. Preferably in another zip code.

He also had some old tools. But not just *any* tools. These were metal-fabricating tools. One was a metal turret lathe. I don't think he even knew how to work it. Anyone who did could have repaired a locomotive. However, knowing how to use your tools is not a prerequisite in the men's zone. They just have to look good.

In one corner was a refrigerator filled with cold long-necked beers and nonalcoholic beers for his buddies who couldn't drink anymore. A Pirelli poster was tacked on the front. A water softener stood nearby. There was also a pool table with a half-built model ship on the worn green felt. And a slot machine that really worked. (Slot machines are contraband in Indiana. All the more reason to keep one around in plain sight.)

A high shelf encircled the room. On display were beer bottles from around the world. Cleaned up. He actually took the time to dust them more than once a decade. In the rafters were rows of boxes, all the same, with perfectly printed labels: "Photos from '61 to '72, summer cottage." Talk about organized!

On one bench was a little AM radio, and a TV with a tinfoil antenna. Clearly, the guy could have afforded any television, but a black-and-white TV is the only thing you can have in a shop. If you can still find one.

His tool bench was an altar to man. The surface was well worn, with nicks and cuts. An old metal vice anchored one end. Half-done projects were strewn everywhere. Probably locomotive parts.

The whole place smelled like a man. In other words, motor oil and solvent—a good cologne, by the way. Depending on where you stood, you could catch whiffs of turpentine, benzine—all the 'zines. Anything caustic to the earth, it was there. Want to melt lead? No problem.

Next to the tool bench was a gun rack. A machine gun from World War Two was the pièce de résistance. And it was loaded, with a big crowbar lock through it.

On the tool pegboard, each tool was outlined. His hammer was even worn out—you don't see that very often. Screws, nuts, and bolts were each in their own plastic drawer, sorted by size and type.

It was all so perfect and so odd: Men can organize a spacious work bench but can't keep poop stains out of their underwear.

My garage is pretty cool, too. It's no Lost City of the Incas, but other guys are jealous. I've got a couple of cars, my tools, and one of those trash cans from the thirties. It's clean as a whistle. I hang out there all summer, with the big door open.

My wife hates it.

"Would you close the door?" she always says.

I prefer that people come into the house *through* the garage.

"People don't enter the house through the garage," she says.

I've always felt safer that way. Because only your friends will do it. Strangers don't go that way. This is one way to tell the difference. When she thinks I'm not looking, she shuts the garage door. I think her real problem is that she doesn't want the neighbors to see what's inside.

I had to tease her. "Good god! They saw the garage! What are we going to do?"

"You think that's funny?" she answered.

"Yes, it's hysterical. But maybe you're right. What if they saw a rake or something in there?"

Not even a smile.

I think she should let me be. I've given her the rest of the house. I even let her design me an office.

She can feel free to use it while I'm in the garage.

One of the newest men's zones is a throwback to the oldest. Thanks to the modern men's movement, guys can once again hang out naked around a roaring fire in the wilderness, chant, and bang on drums until dawn.

In prehistoric times we used to discuss the fine points of buffalo meat, the proper grip for dragging a woman to your cave, and how to distinguish female bloating from overeating. Now, naked in all our flabby, middle-class glory, we come to confess that we didn't get along with our dads, discuss the perfect golf grip, and try to remember how to tell the difference between female bloating and overeating.

I read somewhere that a scientific study determined that all this male sharing is due more to anonymity than to any real sense of bonding. A guy can tell his secrets because he knows he'll never see the other guys again. Well, *of course*. That's male bonding. If you're really curious where your relationship is going with another man, you can always wrestle naked in front of a fireplace like Oliver Reed and Alan Bates did in the movie *Women in Love.*

You'll note that they didn't call the film *Men in Love.*

I don't think the New Age men's-movement trend is going to last very long. If it's good for anything, it's just to keep women on their toes. For some time now men have been insecure and unsure of how to behave in the presence of the new woman. And who says a little confusion isn't good for a woman?

I was reading Robert Bly's book *Iron John* in bed, and my wife cut me down about it. Generally we look at each other's books to see what's interesting our partner lately. But I was all quiet and too engrossed in *Iron John* for her to stand it.

"Ooooh, a story about *men*," she said. "What is it? Some sort of cult?" She was really dogging me. "Is this some kind of men's club you're going to join?" It was as if my reading the book were threatening her.

"No. It's just a book about guys talking about what bugs them."

"What could possibly be bugging you guys?" she said.

I said, "*You* go to the bookstore and it's *full* of women's books.

Help this, help that, help yourself, help her, forget about him. This is just some stupid book about a guy. I didn't even say I liked it."

But she was already mad. The thought that men might be getting together must have scared her.

Not to worry.

The problem is that once these movements become a "thing" they're over with. For a while, in the men's magazines, every other ad was for drums to beat on. "Sign up now for our wilderness weekend. We can get you back to IT."

Business ruins the flavor.

Besides, I've already had my men's-movement weekend. Try driving from Detroit to Indy in the back of a Dodge van with twelve sweaty guys to see a race, singing J. Geils songs, and you'll understand what I mean.

Men like to sit in dark, wood-paneled places, in high-backed chairs, drinking aromatic liquor, and smoking fragrant cigars that smell like the bottom of men's feet. We like to eat salty foods like smoked herring, pistachios, pork rinds, and sometimes just plain salt. All salt does to a woman is make her retain water, which is the last thing she wants. In men's clubs, men do business. Can you imagine a woman wanting to do business when she's bloated?

One great old restaurant in Detroit with a men's-club feel was Carl's Chophouse. Plenty of salesmen went to dinner there. The typical salesman dinner was a porterhouse steak that made the table list to one side, a baked potato, tub o' scotch, no vegetables, plenty of butter, chocolate cake and more scotch for dessert.

Plenty of salesmen died there, too, which gave Carl great pride.

The men's club is a fading tradition. Women want in for some reason, maybe just to prove that we can't keep them out. The club used to be where men would go for a night out when they wanted to be men. Now it's where women can go for a night out when they want to be men. They can have dinner, smoke cigars, drink brandy, do business, and then go to a strip club. Now there are strip clubs for women, too (only they're not as much fun).

As I said previously—but apparently can't repeat often enough—for me, going to a strip club is like going to a restaurant where I can't eat the food. They just bring by big plates of steamed vegetables and beef, and go, "Hey! Don't touch that! You want that to sit down next to you? That's another five bucks. You want me to set it right in front of you and undulate the thing? Twelve-fifty. For twenty dollars, I'll set it in your lap."

Now I play golf. Everyone plays golf now. That is what men used to do, and now they're doing it again. Golf is also a lot like going to a strip club. You get all charged up, pay big money to hang out on a beautiful course, and start drinking early. Eighteen holes later, you're plastered and frustrated, and most of your balls are missing.

Thanks to creeping bizonality, women play golf, too. The only difference between men and women on the golf course is speed. Women don't play as fast as men do, and they get all pissy with us when we express our displeasure at having to stand around while they gently fan the ball. Believe me, we're just thinking about the foursome behind us. Just *hit* it already. I'd play with my wife, but on a big course she'd just take too damn long.

What am I talking about? On a big course, I take too long.

For a man, one of the great pleasures of golfing isn't even on the fairways and greens, or in the bar. The clubhouse locker room is still a pure men's zone. Other guys call you "sir." An obsequious fellow cleans the crud off your golf shoes and clubs. Another shines your street shoes. A gentleman in the bathroom offers an assortment of ointments and tonics, and doesn't ever seem to notice the sounds and smells of your "business" beforehand. And, thank god, there's no place to sit and do your makeup.

The whole area has the funky male smell of washed, wet linen; body odor; sweat; shoe insoles; anti-athlete's-foot powder; and the three primary male aromas: bay rum, Right Guard, and Brut.

Bathrooms at home are nothing like this. Men have to get past the frilly hand towels, lavender soaps, sachet boxes, and baskets full of female hair-care products and facial scrubs, before they can feel comfortable in the can, much less make it their own for a couple of hours.

Women take forever in the bathroom, but they're putting on their makeup. Men can spend all day in the bathroom reading a gun magazine. I read feminist authors, just in case you wondered.

The prison bathroom was pretty damn nice. And convenient. The toilet was right next to the bed. A little stainless-steel affair, but *powerful*. There was none of this "God, I hope that thing disappears." It would suck a blanket down. If you weren't careful, it would suck the air out of the room. We used to start small fires nearby and see if we could put them out just by flushing.

The perfect men's bathroom would be all white tile and the smell of Pine-Sol. There'd be a magazine rack, a window, a stereo system, color TV, and a refrigerator—all of which you could reach without standing up.

And a floor drain.

Women may have green thumbs, but men have traditionally taken care of large plots of land. We had to till the soil and make it do something. Women did the cooking, but men had to feed the family. We evolved from hunters and killers to managing the land. And there's still a little farmer left in every man.

These days we just have to keep the grass short. A real man doesn't hire a gardener, he cuts his own. This takes us to another men's zone: the garden-supply store. That's where you can purchase a tractor mower so big you have to get it smog-tested every two years. That's where you learn to pronounce Briggs & Stratton, mulching blades, vermiculite, John Deere.

All my life I'd dreamed of a John Deere tractor, so I bought a big sucker. They accessorize nicely, too. A $94 option was headlights. Had to have them in case I wanted to mow at night. Hubcaps cost $230. I didn't even have to think about it. I didn't think my wife would think about it either.

I was wrong. Women always notice the accessories.

"You put hubcaps on the tractor!"

"Yeah."

"Why?"

"I don't know, aerodynamics or something."

The truth is that men have few ways to accessorize their lives. We accessorize steering wheels and seat covers in our cars, but that's about it. Women have department stores full of accessories to wander through like Moses in the desert. The volume of accessories available to women is measured in cubic light years. And yet, all a woman needs is new earrings for a whole new look. Same fat head. Same mole on her cheek. But suddenly it's a new look. Men are happy with a new mud guard for the lawn tractor.

The problem is that I don't get to use my tractor too much. Back East people have *lawns*. At my West Coast house, I don't have a lawn. It's more like a salad. I had a salad once at the Palm

Restaurant. I think it cost $400. It looked like my lawn clippings: dandelions, flowers, and grubs.

Back East—where the tractor is—I've got an acre and a half. I grow corn out of my backroom. But I'm not there much. So my step-father, a retired guy, takes care of my lawn when I'm not around. One day I caught him putting up little statues on the lawn and mumbling under his breath. Turns out he was saying crabgrass prayers. Sexually transmitted diseases are easier to deal with than a crabgrass problem.

The only solution to this socially embarrassing situation was to take care of it right, and right away. I hired a lawn service. A big truck pulled up the next day and started spraying stuff on my grass: Chem Grow or Chem Kill, maybe. It could have been iced tea for all I knew. They assured me it was environmentally sound. That's why I didn't understand how come every time I looked out the window there was a *different* guy spraying it? And why was he wearing the full radioactive suit with the little visor?

"What happened to the last guy?"

"Died. But don't worry. This stuff is safe!"

"Is that why my dog's new puppies all have twelve legs?"

"Have you checked the water softener?"

But I didn't care. At least the grass grew. It grew so fast it blew the motor out of my John Deere. Suddenly, I had a John Deere lawn chair.

Downstairs at Sears is a man's home. Craftsman tools are to a man what fine jewelry is to a woman. When I reach the bottom of the escalator and gaze out on those acres of implements, my nipples get rock hard. It's so bright and shiny I have to wear sunglasses in the basement.

Men don't need a reason to buy tools. As long as there's an empty spot on the pegboard, we just have to have them.

There are tools in the Sears basement I've never heard of. What, for instance, is a conduit bender? Oddly enough, it bends conduits.

"No, I don't need a dictionary, I'll just take it."

My Mom said the only reason men are alive is to go to a hardware store or a Sears. I love Sears. I grew up near a Sears. There's a Sears in every town. However, avoid the upstairs at Sears. That's where they have Sears fashion—clearly an oxymoron. Whoever makes their tools evidently also makes their clothes. I make sure my wife buys her fashions at K-Mart.

When I was a kid my mom would punish us by making us go to Sears for dress slacks.

"You've lit your sister on fire for the last time."

"Noooo! I'd rather flatten my balls with a ball peen hammer!"

I never wanted those tough-skin, ugly, double-kneed pants. You could drag behind a bulldozer for six miles on a gravel road on your knees, and it would feel as cool and refreshing as water-skiing. I think they should make postal employees wear Sears fashion as their uniforms.

It could stop bullets, no problem.

Bob Vila once came to my house in Michigan, half crocked out of his mind—just kidding, Bob. We did a project together for his show. I was building a new garage and a family room. His crew wanted to do a run-through, but Bob knew me well enough and said, "Nah." Then we just walked around the project, and he asked, "What are you doing here and here?" I *instinctively* faked it. That is, I did it just the way he would.

"Well, Bob, what we've done here is we've poured our foundation."

He kept trying to throw me off with these big words. "You're using double-ought blah-blah-blah."

I said, "No, we're not. We're using triple." Everything he said I upped it. "How are you heating the place?"

"We're using a coat of low-level uranium six inches underneath the floor. The natural breakdown of reactive materials causes heat."

"Is that a danger to your family?" he asked, with a straight face.

I said, "It's an *unseen* danger. You don't see it, therefore it doesn't exist. Maybe generations from now we'll look like frogs, but now we heat our house for almost five thousand years penny-free."

Then he said, "Wait. There's no basement here."

"You noticed. Actually we built the basement off site," I explained. "We will finish the basement, then lift the entire house and set the basement underneath. I find that cheaper."

This went on for about an hour. As we were talking, my crew finished doing the floor, and then, on nobody's cue, Bob walked right through the wet concrete.

Never trust a TV professional.

Sports are considered by many to be a men's zone. Okay. Fine. But I can't talk about them here. Men and sports are so big it would take seventeen volumes. Also, many guys are so into sports they know statistics about statistics. The only thing I can quote chapter and verse is the Mustang repair manual. I don't even know enough about sports to try and bullshit you.

The only thing I wonder about is the women in the men's locker room thing. What's that all about? Ever see men clamoring to get in the women's locker room? They respect women's privacy in the locker room, unlike some women color commentators who made it a point to go into the men's locker room. Men just wouldn't do that. I just don't think male sportscasters really want to get into the women's locker room to interview naked six-foot-five female basketball players.

On the other hand, I might be totally wrong.

Men are defined by what they do, which is why the classic men's zone is the workplace. We're there all day long. Sometimes we die there, because men do more of the dangerous work. Women blame us for being in control, but we're meaner to ourselves than we are to women. Men work the oil derricks. Men walk the high steel beams. Men repair bridges. Is this by choice or because men are smarter? Or because men are dumber? These jobs don't say to me, "It's a man's world. We run everything." But someone's gotta do it, so the men do. Men take the grungy jobs. If we were really as mean as women say, we'd stay home with the kids and let them enjoy salesman dinners and other industrial accidents.

Attention all women: Men have bosses, too. Men are just as put out by their lack of control as women. I think eight guys—supreme bosses—run everything. Well, I don't know for sure, but this alien who took me into his flying saucer and stuck things up my behind while he examined me—why is it always the rear end? what's up there that's so damn revealing?—told me this as his way of apologizing for my temporarily excruciating discomfort. He's now taken over the body of my family doctor, so I see him a lot. He also told me that no one would believe me—about who really runs the world, I mean.

Whatever women are going through, it's not men's fault. If it is, we sure don't know it. I just thought I'd make that perfectly clear.

Conventional wisdom says that if you want something done well you should do it yourself. So I've decided to design my own amusement park. It will be the ultimate men's zone.

I'll call it Tim Al-Land.

Men are fascinated by, preoccupied with, and genetically predisposed toward two things: Construction and Destruction. Think of the stuff that boys do. Build and destroy. Nothing's changed.

Women are invited to Tim Al-Land, but as with most men's zones, women just don't want to go there. It smells like feet and body odor. It's not real comfortable. It's comfortable *enough*, if you're the kind of guy who likes spending all day on a park bench. It's also chilly all the time, and loud.

Throughout the park there are signs posting rules, which, when broken, earn you a free food ticket. The food pavilions serve the basic men's food groups: meat, carbohydrates, salt, and fat. The hot dogs are rubbery and the potato chips stale. Everything's cooked on a fire and shoved into a casing. All beverages are ice cold. All the tables are tailgates. In the bathrooms there are no toilet seats. But there *is* a recorded voice that cycles through, "Can't you remember to put the seat down when you're through. How hard can it be? I don't find it funny. I almost fell in. . . ." It always gets a big laugh from the married guys. There aren't even any women's bathrooms.

You gotta walk through a big drill to get into Tim Al-Land.

"There's your armature right there. Your pinion's there, son. Stand by the trigger and I'll take your picture."

Inside, you have to wear a vest with lots of pockets. If you forget yours we provide them, just like fancy restaurants when they require coats and ties and you come dressed like a bozo.

As the creator of Tim Al-Land, I suggest the ladies just leave their men at the gate and take advantage of the complete beauty makeover offered at the Tim Al-Land Ladies Annex across the street. Our motto: "We'll make sure it takes hours. And all your girlfriends will be there."

Tim Al-Land: Maybe I can get Disney to do this.

The park reflects the best and worst in man, and is divided into zones. The first is Constructionland.

In Constructionland, you can frame a house. Hell, you can put up a barn. You can lay brick. You can build a bridge. I don't know any guy in the world who wouldn't spend twenty-two bucks for a ticket to run a backhoe all day long. Learn how a front-end loader works. Drive a bulldozer, a grader. You get training in a big gravel pit. Seven bucketloads and you're outta there, so the next guy can get a turn. I once got a letter from some guy who wondered how I'd feel driving the largest front-end loader on the planet Earth. How would I feel lifting thirty thousand pounds of payload, putting it wherever I wanted? I got a chubby just reading the letter.

Next to the gravel pit is a special place where you can use big metal jaws hanging from a crane to try to pick up a car and put it down a little chute. Get it down the chute, it's yours. Damage it and it's yours, too. Of course you damage it!

Even though blowing up things requires the same energy and creativity as building things, Destructionland is clearly the dark side of man.

In Destructionland, a.k.a. Militaryland, men get to use all that Army stuff: machine guns, howitzers, tanks. Only this time they're real. Remember that bridge you built? Blow it up!

My wife would never get inside a tank: "It's so hot in here, it's so cramped. You like this? This is fun for you?"

Every man would be thinking something else entirely: "Will *this* go through that wall?" Soon you're going over a hill at full speed while the barrel's going sideways, firing hot steel.

"Is this the only color? Is it drafty in here? It's so musty. What's that diesel smell?"

In Militaryland you can also sit on the deck of the USS *Missouri*—now decommissioned—and shoot a sixty-inch gun. The shells go twenty miles and, if aimed properly, will obliterate your neighbor's house and leave yours standing.

Of course, my wife would be on the deck going, "It's so loud!"

Me? I'd be half drunk from swilling brown liquor and yelling, "Shoot it again!" The USS *Missouri* would also feature my version of skeet shooting. They fling a little imported car off an island and into the air, and you blow it to bits with a sixty-millimeter. Bang! Bang Bang! Yeah!

In Militaryland you could also take a ride on a Seawolf submarine. Hell, why not water-ski behind it? Think of it: You whiz by the dock, wearing your Sears fashion specials, and wave at everyone. No boat—just you.

A couple of years ago I got to see the USS *Nimitz,* an aircraft carrier. I met the duty-control officer, since promoted to some important liaison job. He was from Down South, and smarter than I'll ever be. But he still sounded dumber than a ham hock.

"That boat five football feels long. Nuklar pawr."

In Militaryland, you could also ski behind the *Nimitz*. You and 3,800 of your favorite friends. Little heads bobbing up and down on the water, trying to keep their tips up. "Hey, Dad!" Takes almost fifteen miles to get her going. "Get your heads up!" Pulls everybody up. "All right!"

There'd always be some bonehead trying to cross the wake. If he falls, everybody has to let go and wait for the captain to yell, "Pull her round again!"

There would have to be some sort of beer pavilion for refreshments. Something with a Bavarian theme, like the Obermeyer Tent. Waitresses in halter tops and lederhosen. Beer steins with relief maps of Italy on them. We could sit around and try to figure out why the Bavarians made cups with metal caps that serve no useful purpose.

After you quench your thirst, it's into the men's room. It's all trough. Forty feet long. The trough of hell. Solid aluminum. Water sloshing through. Eighty guys lined up like horses. And the stalls: no doors, just holes in the floor, like in Italy. No woman would understand it.

Another thing women might be surprised at is that nothing in Tim Al-Land is remotely connected to sex. No way. Sex is not a man's zone. That switches men into another gear. Then they get competitive and fight. That's not cohesion, that's competition. I also figure that unless there's enough to go around, and everyone is happy with what they get—which I don't think is ever possible— then women wouldn't be a good idea. Besides, I'd want to keep all the beer waitresses to myself.

Finally, it's off to Fishingland. Full of fish things. You can see fish, touch fish, kiss fish. Even feel what it's like to be hooked.

"Hold still, kid."

"Oh, god that hurts! Oh, sonofabitch that hurts!"

"Try *that*!"

"Oh, jeez, you're right, that hook really hurts. Isn't that great!" You've got to watch a bass-fishing tournament to really understand the male psyche. I watched one on TNN. It was the seminationals. The contest consisted of teams of two fat guys with double given names—Joe Bob, Ray Bob, Tim Dick—sitting on top of bar stools in a boat made of thirty-five feet of metal-flake fiberglass, powered by an 830-horsepower Mercury motor. Are bass particularly fast little fish? Are Jim Bob and Sam Bob trying to run them down? Do they have to grab them by the head? Why do the boats have to be so fast?

I flew down to Mexico with marlin fishermen once. Now these are big fish. Do you have to eat a piece of marlin to be in this club? Do fishermen even eat fish? I don't think so.

After all the fun at Tim Al-Land, it's finally time to go.

There's a bar next door to the Ladies' Annex where you can grab a beer just in case your wife's hair still isn't done.

But please, no firing the sixty-millimeter guns at the Annex.

What excites me about men is what they can do when they direct their energy. There's nothing more impressive than the things we've built. Environmentally and socially there may be something wrong with the Hoover Dam, but if you look at it and feel the grandeur of it, and realize that *men* designed and built that, it's almost too breathtaking to bear. And the Grand Canyon! Took almost two years—and men did it. And how about the Chunnel, the tunnel between England and France? So what if they missed each other by a few feet trying to meet in the middle? Come on. A few feet in the scheme of things? A little water helps break up the boredom of the drive.

I'll let you in on a secret. All mistakes men make are planned. This gives us a reason to go back to where we live and breathe.

In the men's zone.

more power

If it's got an engine, men love it. If it goes fast, men will figure out a way to make it go faster. Men love anything that makes noise, spins, moves, or smokes. If it's big, make it bigger. If it's loud, make it louder. Men's stuff is always audible. Fishing rods whir. Bolt-action guns "chuck." Cameras click. New stereo equipment sighs. From a toaster to a Stealth bomber, we're always trying to add more power.

Speedintensityvolumepower. Speedintensityvolumepower. The mantra of the modern man.

Men's zones are filled with men's stuff. The whole *world* is filled with men's stuff. I don't know why men *have* so much stuff. Maybe it's because we never listened to our mothers when we were kids. We should have cleaned up our rooms when she told us to.

No wonder the world is one big mess.

Many sociologists, mostly women—okay, only Dr. Joyce

Brothers—have postulated that there are specific reasons why men have so much stuff. I haven't spoken to her personally, so I don't know what these reasons are. However, I believe men's fascination with tools, cars, stereos, computers, and collecting beer bottles from around the planet stems from the creation urge. Men can't have babies, so it's our way of feeling important and useful. This, more than an inherent fascination with socket wrenches, is what makes us want to crawl under the car and restrut the suspension, or change the oil every three thousand miles, and not mind when big globs of filthy petroleum product land smack on our foreheads. This urge to control *something* is what draws us to a shoeshine kit full of black, brown, and cordovan polish; and brushes and rags caked with spittle.

Having mentioned shoes, here's a question that's always nagged me: What is it with women and shoes, anyway? Women don't seem to realize that they can actually polish shoes *in the home*. They get a scuff and the shoes are as good as garbage. It's time to go shopping for another pair. If we could redirect the money spent on overpriced women's footwear, we could halve the national debt. Women have fifteen pairs of shoes in the closet, and that's just in black. There are slant-back heels, half heels, spikes, pumps, espadrilles, and shoes that don't even look like shoes.

Don't tell me that being able to have babies eradicates all of women's compulsions.

For instance, the purse thing. Women have sixty purses, and I've still got the same wallet I made in camp.

There's not a man I know who would purposely look in a woman's purse. Purse snatchers learn this early. Grab the purse, dump the lipstick, earrings, cosmetics, tampons, datebook, car keys, combs and brushes, diet energy bars, sleeping bag, pup tent, Miata. Get the money. I've never looked in a woman's purse. Never opened one. A real man doesn't go into a purse. It's a no-man's-land. You can lose yourself in that thing. My wife once discovered $300 in her purse that she'd misplaced. How do you do that? I can understand misplacing the money, but in your own purse? But she looked in her purse and there it was, right next to the antique dresser.

My wife and I went to Florence, Italy, recently. She said she wanted to see Michelangelo's David and other classic works of art. She didn't tell me she'd discovered that Florence is where the purse was invented. We went shopping ten minutes after we'd checked into our hotel. They've got two streets of shops that just sell *brown* purses. My wife's eyes left their sockets! And then she was gone. I followed her into a store and there she was, "trying on a purse!"

"Just buy them all," I said. "We've got stuff to do. Great art to see."

"The David's waited this long," she said. "I don't think he's getting off his pedestal and going anywhere for the next couple of days. Besides, these purses are on sale and they're Italian. Now how 'bout this clutch? Too clunky?"

What could I say? My wife is just as confused when I try to explain why I need another tool I'm never going to use.

Meanwhile, she's modeling purses and I'm fighting off narcolepsy. I can't shop with women. I just get tired. I walk into the women's wear department of any store and my energy just goes to hell. I'm suddenly seven and in the backseat of the family station wagon, being lulled to sleep by the hum of the road. There's something about fluorescent lights in malls that makes me very weak. It's like they're made of kryptonite. (However, fluorescent lights in electronics stores make me feel suddenly energetic.) Women know this. That's why, instead of letting you go off and do your own shopping, they make you sit in those little student punishment seats by the dressing rooms. Then they waltz out in some god-awful froufrou and say, "What do you think?"

You muster the stock answer. "Nice. Very nice." And then you follow with the appropriate shared "nod and smile" to the exhausted husband in the other chair.

Then she disappears and returns with a cocktail purse that matches the outfit. It's about the size of a maraschino cherry and *it costs $3,000*. At that price it should match any outfit. It just carries itself. Oh—and you can't fit anything in it.

"It's *supposed* to be decorative, honey."

Oh, the things you want to say, but don't.

I love cars. Cars are my life. My wife is a bright corporate lady who could care less about cars. When we could finally afford to buy her any car she wanted, I asked her to reveal to me her heart's desire. Anything, anything, any-thing . . ."

"Red," she said.

Boys fantasize about cars because cars mean only one thing: extending boundaries way past home. They represent adventure. You can drive across country. You can get out of town. Cars are freedom. Guys want power. Freedom is power. (Like most kids, I also fantasized about being a superhero. I liked Spiderman. And what did I want to use my new superpowers for? To get a car. That's me. Lofty goals.)

Women have a much more subtle approach to cars and the freedom they represent. Mainly, how to get in and out gracefully. How to dress so the guys with the cars will give them rides. The social niceties. They assume they'll be *in* cars, but they already know it's to their advantage not to *own* a car because of the equity problem, depreciation, and, with the exception of race driver Shirley "Cha Cha" Muldowney, they probably can't fix it, nor do they want to. Women are right to think that it's easier just to get someone to be the mechanic and chauffeur them around. This, next to having children and garbage removal, is the reason most women want husbands.

I like cars so much I'd hang around parking lots if I didn't think someone would call the police. I once went to a store to get wheel covers for my car, because someone had stolen them, and I could have spent the day there. When I drove in, a guy just getting out of his car at the same time said, "Nice wheels." In guy talk, that meant he thought I was a nice guy.

"What you got under the hood?" (He wants to know more about me.)

"Supercharged hemi." (I'm a forward thinker, a risk taker.)

"Where do you redline?" (Depends on what he is referring to.)

"Seven thousand rpm. Tops out around 140 mph." (I'm way too fast for you, buddy. But thanks for asking.)

One thing I'll always like about living in Los Angeles is that everybody has a car. Everyone *has* to have a car. Otherwise you've got to train for the marathon just to get some milk at the grocery store. Some of the homegrown custom-car designs are a little tough to understand, though. Who came up with the idea of taking those teeny, tiny, mini pickup trucks with the little motors, and fitting them with huge tires and sound systems so loud I think we're having an earthquake aftershock every time a cruiser drives up my street?

Then there's the L.A. obsession with sports utility vehicles. Where I grew up, near the Rocky Mountains, we didn't have four-wheel drive. Just chains. Now everyone's got a Range Rover to announce their ability to rough it in style. It's now acceptable, even trendy, to answer the question "Do you do much offroading?" with "Nope. But I can if I ever want to." Or "What's offroading?" I was driving down the street and this guy in the Range Rover next to me was talking on the cellular phone, faxing something to his office, watching the ball game on his Sony mini TV, and making love to some woman. I think it was just his way of saying, "Look at me!

Look at me!" I looked, but I still can't figure out who was driving the car.

The old Toyota Landcruiser was a real man's car. It looked functional. Now it's all styling. Range Rover makes a vehicle that looks like it's right out of *Daktari*. It's got a lion or an elephant guard on it. As soon as I saw it, I wanted one. I'd also love a Humvee, like Ah-nold. "Maria. We will take the Hummer!" Anytime they make something that looks like it came from the military, you know lots of men are thinking, "Yeah, I like it." There's a purpose to military stuff that's attractive. It strikes deep into the core of man. And it's spread beyond the barracks. Construction equipment is built using the same principles of massive power and indestructibility. Except for the yellow color, I wouldn't mind owning a bulldozer. Drab olive is better. Everything looks better in drab olive, even bedsheets. One day I'll have a car that's flat green from bumper to bumper. And I won't wash it. The look will improve with age. Pretty soon the neighbors will be asking each other, "Did a bush with a gun barrel on it just go by here?"

One good thing about my car obsession is that I can fix my own vehicle. Or I could, until I got a Cadillac with the Northstar engine system. If the first scheduled maintenance isn't until 100,000 miles, why should I mess with it? There's probably a federal law against tampering with this engine. I was looking under the hood a couple of days ago and I found one of those tags like they have on mattresses, sticking out from under the windshield-wiper-solution container. It said, "We don't care if you remove this tag, but don't even think about touching *anything* else."

I have a couple of different dream cars. One is a maxed-out Mustang that I helped design myself. I'd also love to own a Ferrari. I don't know what it is about them. I've wanted a black Ferrari since I was a kid. Do you think it's a coincidence that Testarossa sounds a lot like testosterone? I don't know if I'd ever be able to drive a Ferrari anywhere, though. I'd just feel like a stupid middle-class guy, driving down the boulevard, trying to talk on the cellular, fax the office, watch TV, and make love to my wife, all without running a red light or annoying the guy in the Range Rover next to me.

Another vehicle I dream of owning is a long-distance cruiser that's a cross between a van, a Mercedes, and a Corvette. It would have seats like an airplane so you could sleep, or kick the guy in front of you when he pushes the recline button and his tray table jams you in the balls. It could go off road, fly, dive underwater, and be totally self-contained. I could live in it if the wife kicked me out. It would even be outfitted with metal-fabricating tools so I could make my own parts if the vehicle broke down. And I could drive forever, never take a bath, and eat candy all day.

Why do men like tools and stuff? Lots of people think it's social imprinting. I think they mean that schools make boys go to shop class and the effects are permanent. I'd rather have been in home economics—though I've yet to meet a woman who took that class who can discuss international monetary funds and World Bank theory with me—much less know what it really means to be economical. Those lifetime disappointments notwithstanding, even back in school it was already clear that girls and food are better than bending metal or making arty ashtrays.

Every shop class was the same. You never got anything done. There were so many rules and regulations for guys.

"Get your tool, stand by your stations, wait for instructions."

"Follow the yellow line back to your stations, begin your projects."

Five minutes later the warning bell rang.

"All right, go back to your stations, clean your tools, and get the hell out of my sight."

The shop teacher always wore a lab coat. I once saw a movie where a chimp wears a lab coat. That made about as much sense as Mr. Johnson pretending to be a professional. All my shop instructors were missing fingers, too.

"You gotta watch that circular saw, that baby'll kick back on you. I'm not joking around! Now somebody help me pass out these test papers."

Like I said, I'd rather have listened to a home ec. teacher with burnt flambé all over her face. "Girls, watch those flambés, they'll blow up. Look at these scars, I'm not fucking around!"

The problem with tool belts is butt cracks. The older journeymen wear suspenders. Young guys—you know, I think they *like* that butt crack. My brother is a contractor in Kalamazoo, he does apartments. When he and his contractor friends get together it looks like a butt-crack festival. These guys *gotta* know what they're showing. Plumbers, because of the positions they've got to assume when working, have the worst butt-crack problem in the world.

"Hey, Tony, look at that crack, that's gotta be eight inches."

"Uh huh. Pretty great, right?"

"Why don't you just wedge the house plans in there and walk 'em over to the supervisor?"

"Pete! Nice butt crack. What's that—a pencil holder back there?"

"Nice. But I brought my little girl and she's eating over here.

How about I spackle that son of a bitch shut? I got some DAP latex butt-crack filler, how 'bout I run a bead of caulk down that fat ass of yours so she can keep her food down?"

Butt crack is like male cleavage. I'd like to design a line of drop jewelry for men. Butt-crack ornamentation. Pearls and gold coins to enhance the natural lines. Pretty soon pants will be cut low for the more daring male, and "elective crack surgery" will be the latest craze. Now *there's* a "before and after" album I wouldn't like to see displayed in a plastic surgeon's office. I'm making myself sick.

I love tool belts, though, despite their shortcomings. Unfortunately, the perfect tool belt hasn't yet been invented. So I have three: a carpenter's, a general handyman's, and a barbecue belt. The last has a spatula, fork, and poker all on chains. You pull 'em out and they snap back. It's got ketchup, mustard, and Tabasco in little cases. My wife knows I'm not just whistling Dixie when I'm wearing all three—naked—in the bedroom.

The ultimate belt wouldn't be a belt at all. It would be something designed by Porsche, Mercedes, Bosch, Black and Decker, Motorola, and Q, from the James Bond movies. You'd carry it in a little shoulder holster. It would be a little silver thing, all polished stainless steel, that contained a drill, saw, shaper, and glue gun. And it would be rechargeable. The Swiss army knife of tools.

But for now, I'm pretty fond of my handyman's belt. It's a big, fat strip of cowhide, with huge pockets and loops. I walk around with two Makitas slung low, like six-shooters.

"Come on, honey. Break something. I dare you."

I walk around the house looking for things to rewire. I fixed Grandpa's hearing aid once because he kept saying "What?" every time I spoke to him. It was nothing, really, to give it more power. I stopped by Radio Shack, got some coaxial cable, a 160-watt preamp, with Dolby. Gramps can hear fine now. On a clear night he can also pick up space-shuttle transmissions.

I bought a Makita mini circular saw. I just had to have it. I've used it once. However, my wife has used it a number of times, but never for its intended purpose, which is cutting wall paneling on the job site. You make little notches, then cut in and cut out. She uses it at home, blows the blade off, and says, "This thing doesn't work right."

"Well, honey, I'm not sure that you're supposed to use it to cut hair or chicken parts."

With some prodding she eventually started using my full-size circular saw. It's hell on hair, but cutting the chicken is a snap. Cutting the chicken's hair takes practice.

As you've probably guessed, I get asked tool, construction, and repair-related questions all the time by people who somehow have the idea that I know what I'm talking about. Here are a couple of the most popular. I take no responsibility if you follow any of my advice, or believe a word of what I say. I'm warning you now.

Q: Does a guy really need a wrench set with twelve double-headed crescents, twenty sockets and driver, and ten Allens (no relation)?

A: You don't. I've got a multihead driver now that replaces everything in my toolbox. If I could only figure out how to work it. It's heavy and it clicks and it's substantial—which, for me, is half the reason to buy it—but it just sits there. Good thing I've got the old wrench set.

Q: Why do some screws have one-slot heads and others have cross-hatched Phillips heads? And who is Phillips, anyway?

A: Never met the guy. But someone told me that his misshapen head comes to a point, but folks don't dare talk about it since the murder—yes, with a screwdriver. Guess he's related to the milk of magnesia family. (What the hell is a magnesia and how do you milk it?) This seems reasonable since you need some milk of magnesia to calm your stomach after spending all day trying to get a Phillips-head screw out of the wall after you've stripped the slots in the first two minutes. And here's some more bad news. Now the hardware stores feature something called the star-pad screw. The screw head is indented in the shape of a five-pointed little twinkler. Now all the manufacturers are using it, which means that five billion screwdrivers are obsolete. Don't you wish you'd thought of that!

Q: What's the weirdest tool you ever bought?

A: Actually, it was a garden shredder. A garden machine, but still a tool, right? It was a major deal. A freight company had to deliver it to my door. A big diesel Kenworth pulled up in front of my house and two burly guys hauled the shredder off the truck. The thing has a twelve-horsepower motor, and is all tricked out. Here's what it does: It grinds up wood *right on your property.*

Don't laugh. (Okay, my wife did, too.) I just wanted to get rid of all the twigs that had gathered during the year on my little acre-and-a-half. I've got a lot of big trees and they're always shedding. The guy made it look so easy on the commercial; his hair never moved. After using the shredder, the young couple on TV put the grounds in a blender and made mulch. They smiled all the while. You're supposed to put it on your junipers and related bushes. Unfortunately, I almost lost a leg trying to start the shredder because it was so powerful. And then it made so much noise just running I thought it was broken. So I got scared. All I could visualize was an index finger getting caught on one twig and then sucking me in like a guy who gets too close to the jet intake on an F-14. My wife told me she wasn't looking forward to tending to my bloody stump just because I wanted to occasionally *see* the lawn. She also thought I was indulging in a little overkill.

"Aren't you using an atomic bomb to kill a mosquito?" Always

,so quick with a metaphor. "Just wrap up the twigs, take them to the street, and let the garbage man pick them up. I'm quite certain he won't break your leg or bloody your body. Better yet, burn them. That means you get to play with fire!" She sure knows how to push my buttons.

It was good advice. Now the shredder is moldering in the shed, right next to the lawn tractor I don't use anymore.

Q: How would you reinvent classic household tools?

A: I'd like to have an upright cordless vacuum cleaner. Also, a washing machine that lets you know when to put in the fabric softener. Not that I've ever vacuumed or done the laundry. I'd do it, though, if they'd design an iron, or a washing machine, or a clothes drier that a man would like. I don't need floral patterns, mushrooms, or birds on everything. I'm not even sure women do.

Q: Can you explain why plugs now have one prong bigger than the others, and can I alter the big one by hand at home and still use it safely?

A: It's all about polarities, to make all current run in the same direction. There's a big danger in alternating current. If you cross too many currents it will short out the whole system—possibly the planet. So they designed the new plugs to keep everything running in the same direction. I'm not sure I believe this, though. In fact, I 'd like to know who gave them permission to change the plug, and maybe make one of his nostrils just a little bit bigger than the other.

On three-pronged plugs, the round prong is the ground. The most serious electrical problem in America is having an appliance or a computer with a three-pronged plug and only two-pronged holes to plug it into. Just what are you going to do? Those little gray adapter plugs never stay in the wall. Plus they look ugly. So you go through a big guilt trip wondering if you should cut off the fat bastard.

"Nobody's watching. There's no cops here. What would happen if I just sliced that sucker right off?"

I'd do it, but I'm still under the impression that somewhere in your neighborhood's power plant is one gauge designed to monitor this particular problem, that goes like this: "What th—? Some idiot snipped off that ground plug! All points bulletin. Send a squad car to Allen's house! We'll scare the crap out of him and he'll never do it again."

Good thing the first offense is only a misdemeanor, though I hear that if you cut off three prongs you're out.

I've never clipped the ears off the big-sided prong. I bought a grinder to do that.

Q: What else would you like to improve around the house besides the plugs?

A: I wish the home's control center was more visible. I want more access to plumbing. And electrical wiring shouldn't be quite so hidden. My house wouldn't be real pleasant to look at; it would seem more like a submarine than a home, but I think there's a way you make the mechanics of the house more functional and still live with it.

I told the guy who's building a house for me my concerns. He said, "I can make this look like an office building if you want."

Yeah, that's *just* what I meant.

Q: You're so manly. What are you really good at around the house?

A: Mostly just hanging pictures. It's good work, a steady job. I use a hammer, and on special occasions a level. It's real exciting.

Q: Do you mind it when complete strangers ask you for home-improvement advice?

A: A pilot did once. He knew I was on the flight and he came back to the passenger section from the cockpit. I saw him and my first thought was "Oh god. Please let the autopilot be on." Then he stared at me for a few seconds, trying to make up his mind about something, and I thought, "No, don't let him tell me that there's only one guy aboard who can land this 757, and that would be me."

Finally, he sat down, and from the corner of his mouth he said, "If my stucco went all the way down to the foundation and I was getting a leak, would I . . ." I cut him off. Then I said, "What would *you* do?" Letting him figure things out for himself was my best option since I had no idea what the hell he was talking about.

When it comes to more power, you can always find it on late-night infomercials. And it's *always* something we've never heard about before in America but is supposed to be really huge in Europe.

If it's so great, why *haven't* we heard of it? And how come they're reduced to selling it with infomercials? How come the retail stores aren't lining up to get their hands on the newest miracle product? Is the phrase "not available in stores" something that is supposed to entice me? Is it better if it's available on the street corner? How come I'm supposed to always beware of imitations? How come they're always limited time offers? No wonder I have anxious bowel syndrome.

This reminds of the Psychic Hot Line, also advertised via infomercial. "Want to know the future, call the hot line. Your own personal psychic is waiting for your call." Yeah, right. When I call, I never tell them my name. Let them tell me! Most infomercials rely on the Boxcar Willie syndrome. *He's* huge in Europe but no one's ever heard of him here. I don't even know who he is! But if all of Europe (and remember, Hungary and Bulgaria are also part of Europe) is wild about a car wax that protects your car's finish so well that you can light a fire on the hood and leave no marks, you've got to wonder if we've even been talking to Europe lately. Phone lines down? Have we not communicated with these people for months at a time?

Here's what I think. In Europe, the infomercials say the product is bigger than Moses in America. And the truth is that we have warehouses full of some crap we bought in Taiwan and can't get rid of.

The last time I bought anything by mail was from the Sears catalog. I could trust them. But now the catalog is gone. Too bad, since they had everything in there, including beekeeping equipment. Sounds just like a company that kept good tabs on their customers' needs.

Actually, I did buy one tool from a TV ad. I've never taken it out of the box, though. So does that count? From what I could see on the infomercial, the thing is a wonderful tool, so practical it has a thousand and one uses—but I've never been able to get it out of the box. Guess I need one of those tools to help. I hear it gets into tight places that no screwdriver could ever fit.

My favorite is the magical lubricant that the hucksters spray on the sparkplugs and distributor cap of a running engine. Then they turn a fire hose on the engine. Most engines will stop dead if you drive through a puddle fast enough. But this thing just kept running.

How come we don't know about this? Has anybody told the drivers at Indy? Hell, I'm going to call NASA myself.

Real men get really dirty, and they need something strong to clean up with. I like Lava soap, the soap for men. Lava can wash those grease-stained palms and hairy arms and filthy fingernails. There's also Go-Jo, that cream auto mechanics use. Wipe it on—you don't need water—and wipe it off with a rag. I think it works by removing the top layer of skin. Yet it's easy on your hands because it's made with lanolin. I know lanolin comes from sheep. (Do sheep know lanolin comes from sheep?) I think Go-Jo, is made from the whole animal ground up. It's full of oil and it's got a really bad odor. But it works, and with an ounce of imagination, it makes you feel like a real mechanic. Go-Jo will take off anything, including chrome. It also works wonders making French fries.

Jerky, from a cow, a buffalo, even a turkey, is nature's most perfect food. Beef jerky is a grown-up's V-8 juice. It makes you feel like a real cowboy. I reach for my jerky when I want something not sweet but substantial. Which reminds me of a story.

I once met a guy in a club in Texas who had shot a boar. Shooting it was illegal, but he said it had come after his dog. It was probably more like "Honey, let the dog out now, okay?"

Once it was good and dead, he brought the boar to the club, wrapped in towels. Why he'd want to use his wife's nice red towels to wrap a boar, I don't know, but from the look on his face when he slapped it down on the table, it was clear that if I didn't eat some, he'd think I was a puss, and he'd slap me. "You want a bite of it now? It's a fine taste."

"Uh—yeah. Sure."

And I ate it. It was possibly the finest taste I'd ever had in my life. I was rolling it around in my mouth when he looked me straight in the eye and said, "You don't think I'd bullshit an *entertainer*, do you?"

My first thought was that he was just waiting for me to fall to the ground and hold my stomach so that he could say, "I hate guys like you."

And now excuse me a second.

"Honey, let the dog out now."

The Victoria's Secret catalog is one of the finest modern-day examples of men's stuff. Why some people think it's women's stuff, I don't know.

Men are very different around women than they are around themselves. Imagine four guys—with their wives—looking at the Victoria's Secret catalog.

"That would look good on you, honey."

"That's a nice uh . . . what do you call that thing?"

"A camisole."

"Yeah. Yeah. It's you, honey. How about if we order that?"

"How sweet! Give me your credit card."

Now: four guys by themselves:

"Wow. What I could do with her."

"Wish my wife looked like that."

"That bustier is tighter than my . . . oh, oh, here come the girls. Honey, hi. Isn't this a great look?"

"Just give me your credit card and I won't say another thing."

The Victoria's Secret catalog revolution happened quickly and quietly. It just took off. No Morality First groups complained about its being too sexy or pornographic like some other magazines. It goes through the U.S. mails without a hassle. Every guy knows the models' names by heart. This is one reason that men, no matter how much they hate shopping with their wives or girlfriends, are always willing to make an exception and stop by the Victoria's Secret store at the mall. Never seem to feel sleepy there.

You never know when Jill Goodacre will pop by.

If men have tools, so do women.

Women as a rule have different priorities. Their tools come in a cosmetics box, which is just a fishing-tackle box, only for women. Operating on the "real men don't *ever* look in a woman's purse" principle, I've never snuck at peek in a woman's cosmetic kit. I'm afraid of what I'd find. Shampoo, combs, and brushes are no big deal, but what's that scissor thing with a half moon of foam on it. I've seen one lying around, but I still can't figure out what it's for. Taking the eyeball out and dusting or something? Don't fiddle with women's stuff when they're not around, either.

"What happened to my eyeliner pencil? Did you touch it?"

"Ohhh. The phone rang, I couldn't find anything else to write with. It's just a pencil, I'll go replace it." Thirty-eight bucks and a decent command of the French language later . . .

Epilady is a woman's tool that has always confused me. The only thing louder than that machine is her screams as it rips the hair from her body. It was the most returned gift ever at Kmart. And they took it back, though they don't generally take personal-hygiene products back—for good reason. But women had no idea how rough the Epilady was. And when they found out, and tried to give it to their husbands, there were no takers.

"No thanks. I'd rather not *rip* the hair off my face. I'm going to need it again tomorrow."

Note: Don't put women's underwear on your head and run around making faces. If you must experiment, try it when she's gone. You can look in the mirror longer, and you're much freer to express yourself. I recommend her bikini briefs, ears through the holes, and going nuts to the Tijuana Brass *Whipped Cream on Top* album. You know the green cover with that naked girl hidden by Reddi Wip? Oh, and for god's sake be sure to pull the shades. Wow. I was just making that stuff up. You didn't think that I . . . I was just saying that. I don't do that. Unless you do that. Do you do that? If you do that, then I may have done that once—or twice. Unless you haven't. Then I was just kidding.

Women use stuff like concealer powder. Lamb placenta. Lamb placenta from Estee goddamn Lauder. I'm guessing it's lamb placenta from a lamb, but they know best.

"It's from Europe!"

"Yeah. I'll bet it's the rage in Bulgaria." Now there's an attractive bunch of women.

I can't buy my wife anything without gems in it anymore. Often she tells me to buy her stuff that I'd want to see.

"We've been married for years. Just use your instinct."

So I bought her a bench grinder. That pissed her off.

"Well, if you're not going to use it, I'll just store it in my shop." I wanted to smooth things over, so I got her a scissors sharpener from QVC: "It eliminates the worry of sharpening scissors at home!" When I heard that, I was half drunk with anticipation. My Visa card was so excited it dialed the 800 number itself. Now that I can sharpen all my scissors, I'll save all that time. I'd forgotten that I'd never sharpened a pair in my life! I've got the same bent-up pair I had in high school. When I was little, my mom had some *good* scissors in a little velvet case, in the safe-deposit box. She put them there after I tried to use them to trim my little brother's ear lobes.

She caught me and screamed: "Don't touch the good scissors for god's sake. They're from Europe!"

Some people think a vibrator is the ultimate women's tool. Not me. I think women would rather have lipstick than a vibrator. Lipstick makes them look pretty. A vibrator just makes them look scary. I'm a little suspicious of those neck vibrators and body massagers I see in the gift catalogs. Why do they list them by inches: seven, nine, eleven. Isn't that just a little odd? Even so, I've never heard of a big run on vibrators. But a new shade of lipstick, with a $30 "free" makeup-kit gift with purchases of $6,000 or more. This is what women want. A tip: Stay away from department stores during cosmetic specials. It would hurt less to be run over by a buffalo stampede.

I once went to Sears to buy a workbench. I thought it was about time. Sears had a sale on. It came in a big, big box and there was some assembly required. There were instructions, but I didn't need those. Hey, I'm a guy; my balls will tell me how it all fits together. At that point in my life I didn't have many tools except those in a telephone drawer by the kitchen phone. Unfortunately, something was stuck in the drawer and I couldn't open it. Finally, I heard a snap, and the drawer opened. Inside was a picture of another family. Also, pens that didn't work, broken rubber bands, seven batteries. Four are good, three are not, and you will never figure out the combination.

Clearly I needed some tools, so it was back to Sears. I had to buy so many tools that I didn't want to make two trips. So I rented a Ryder truck. I backed that big diesel turbo up to the loading dock and hauled out half the tool-department stock. Now I got your needle-nosed, vice-grippin' monkey's mother, three-quarter drive and socket-pulling, inside-outside torque jig rip cross . . . Yeah, I got myself some tools. Tools that fix tools. Most of them rubber-coated for safety. And duct tape. No shop in America is complete without ninety feet of three-inch-wide U.S.-made duct tape. The silver kind. My wife thinks it looks good across my mouth, too. Matches her jewelry. My motto: If you can't fix it, duct it!

My mom once gave me a gas grill, a Sunbeam 3200. Dual burners, rotisserie grill, pull-down serving area, and in a handy garden cart. But it came unassembled. It looked like a car bomb.

I decided to build it right in the living room and give the whole family a chance to participate. Besides, the light was better indoors and I was flying on pure instinct. Who'd have thought there'd be any grease involved in the process? Every guy's been where I've been. You finish building it, it looks great, but there's a weird bag of important-looking stuff left over.

"Honey? Why don't *you* try the grill out first? I'll be in the basement with my welding hat on."

She pushed it out onto the deck and lit it up. Suddenly the place looked like a nuclear test site. Whoosh!

"Ahhhhhhhh!"

"Honey, run toward my voice!

"Running just makes the flames hotter!"

"That means this thing that's left over is a fuel regulator! Not supposed to spray your hair like that. Guess I don't need to tell you, do I? Why don't ya come in and I'll put some salve on that for ya."

The thing I like most about men's stuff, from tools to stereos, is that your presence affects your possessions. When they glitch, it's probably because you're in a hurry or a bad mood. I've got two TVs at my house that, if I'm in a real bad mood, don't turn on. I called Sony about it. The man says, "I wouldn't touch it if you're in *that* mood. Don't go near your stereo either."

I decided to also avoid the houseplants.

This is when you finally realize that guy stuff has gotten stupid. It should have been easy to tell the first time I had to read the VCR instruction book more than I got to watch videotapes. And another weird thing. In my video room it's always twelve o'clock.

When men's stuff starts affecting the time zones, you *know* it's time to spend more time with your family.

masculinism

Like most men, I'm confused by feminism. It also confuses many women, but that's someone else's book. For the longest time I wasn't sure what the word actually meant. At first I thought it was "the study of what men do wrong." That was because many of the loudest early voices in feminism seemed to be man haters. They didn't like us. They said we'd screwed up everything. They thought the planet would be better off without us. When they were feeling generous, they might say that men were only good for one thing, and that we weren't very good at that, either. I don't know why, but I took that personally.

Feminism has grown a lot since then. Most women don't think men should be exterminated. They'd be satisfied if we agreed to submit our brains to a good housecleaning—and if we'd hire an undocumented alien to do it, and remember to pay her social security taxes.

I've always wanted to understand feminism, so I tackled a regimen of intense research into the subject. Eventually, I earned a

Ph.D. in Advanced Women's Studies, by correspondence course. All it took was one of my days off after the TV season wrapped, before I went on the road, wrote this book, and made a movie. I now realize that *feminism* describes an ideology with an ongoing agenda to support women's self-image, to create equality in the workplace, and to provide more choice in all areas of life. In short, as former NOW Chairwoman Patricia Ireland has said, feminism's goal is to promote the recognition of this simple fact: Women are people, too.

Unfortunately, there is no related expression or ethos—no opposite of feminism—to bind men together. Hmmm. Some would say that men don't need that sort of thing because we already own everything. We run everything. We have the best jobs. We get to do whatever we want, whenever we want. We don't *need* a philosophy for being on top. Men are pigs. R-R-R. Well, bullshit. I think a lot of men don't enjoy, take advantage of, or even recognize their alleged superiority.

Nonetheless, I thought men should have a credo, so I checked around. I read all the great social philosophers. I hung out in leather bars. I looked in the dictionary for a term that might define us. The only word that came close was "philanthropist," which means "love or benevolence toward mankind, in general." Of course, that definition has been obsolete since women joined mankind about thirty years ago, with the advent of feminism. Still, the definition includes the idea that a philanthropist is someone who makes an "effort to promote the happiness or social elevation of mankind, by making donations." This can get pretty confusing. A philanthropist is a lover of man, but a feminist isn't a lover of women. *That's* a "philanderer," which conveniently comes right before philanthropy in the dictionary. A philanderer is someone who "makes love without serious intentions."

I don't know anything about that—or putting underwear on my head.

A good friend was helping me search dictionaries for answers, and finally he said, "Clearly, you've discovered an epistemological void." I didn't even want to look up that word. I was afraid it might have something to do with men's bathrooms or something I should see my doctor about.

I've taken enough abuse without having to look stupid, too.

Finally, after lots of deep, hard thinking in the only place a man can get a little peace of mind, I realized I had no choice but to coin my own term so that men didn't feel left out.

I call it "masculinism."

Feminism celebrates female traits. Masculinism celebrates male traits. They collide to create the volatility of life. The *Sturm und Drang*. The exquisite passions. The troublesome tensions. The family fights about who takes out the garbage and who drives the garbage truck.

The differences are so much more vast that bookstores are stocked with volumes lamenting the sorry state of intersexual relations, because men and women just don't understand each another. Writer after writer has tried to explain this state of affairs, and the illicit affairs that result. Writer after writer churns out books knowing the female market for self-help is seemingly bottomless.

I'm tired of waiting for the compleat man-woman dictionary. I guess I'll have to do that myself.

To some, the distinctions between the sexes—their attitudes, sexual styles, communication skills, and personal hygiene habits—are unsolvable conundrums, destining men and women to be forever at odds.

Sounds about right.

Masculinism and feminism embody those differences. We hate them, we love them, we can't do much about them. So we might as well enjoy them.

After all, they're pretty darn entertaining.

Men are pigs. We all know it. And the odd thing is that men don't seem to mind it when I say so. There's not much you can call a guy that gets him upset. At least not after we've endured the way men have been portrayed on TV sitcoms for over forty years. Television berates us and we take it. We're thought of as dumb slugs. Idiots. This is troubling since for a long time men also wrote, produced, and directed most television. Maybe we were feeling guilty.

But I don't think so. When I call men pigs, they go, "Yeah, we are!" We just don't speak up when the tube is putting us down. Instead, we use it as an excuse for even more odd behavior. So sue me.

Culture—okay, women—can demean men all they like, but just ask yourself who built the computer I'm writing this book on?

This question supports a prime masculinist theory: If women are always complaining about men, tell me who raised the men? Women made us what we are. If women want to take credit—and it's due—for all their hard work of staying at home and raising the kids (a job deserving high pay), they should also accept the responsibility for strongly influencing the boys who largely create and dominate culture.

Women are lateral thinkers. They have communities. They share information and help one another. They listen. At least that's what I thought I heard someone say once.

Men don't listen, particularly to women. This shouldn't be a big surprise. A woman will talk and talk and talk about some problem until a man cuts her off and says, "Here's what I'd do." Men are always giving advice out of their own experience. Men think vertically. Some guy is always bigger, badder, better. His car is nicer, his job more lucrative, his women prettier. Men live to vanquish those challenges. They don't mind helping a woman overcome her problems, if only she'll listen. Men want women to get on with their lives, so that they can go back to watching *Combat* reruns.

Women don't *want* to hear our advice. They don't want solutions to their crises. They just want an arm around their shoulders and a soft-spoken "I understand. I feel the same way!" This is why women are better off being miserable in groups. Suffering doesn't seem to matter to women as long as they don't have to suffer alone.

If that's what women want, I'm not going to try to change them. After all, men are even bigger babies in the suffering department, especially when we're sick. However, I suspect women like that position of power. Besides, when they're in the next room, they can't hear our whimpers and moans too clearly.

"Tim? Did you say something?"

"Ohhhhhhh. Gaaack!"

"Just try and get some rest, dear."

If I could change one thing about women it would be to stop them from mumbling when they walk around corners. They should finish conversations while they're looking at you.

"Oh, by the way mumble, mumble . . ."

"Yeah, yeah, the most important thing is mumble, mumble."

My wife does this all the time, then she's gone. A week later she looks at me like I just killed a kitten and says, "I *told* you all about that." And I can't say she didn't, I just didn't hear it.

"I told you yesterday."

"Yeah, but I was outside!" Actually, I was in the car, with the windows closed, leaving the driveway. She was standing in the doorway, and her lips were moving. I thought she was saying, "You're a man's man. Hurry back. I've got a big surprise for you in the bedroom."

What she was really saying was, "And make sure you bring back some milk."

Why do women do all the sewing, while men are the tailors? Why are women the cooks, but men the chefs? When women remove stains, it's from shirts, pants, and carpets. When men remove stains, it's from granite façades, the Statue of Liberty's skin, or—ahem—spray paint off a high school wall. When women clean, they use Pledge and wear yellow plastic gloves. When men clean they use sand and steam and wear yellow plastic protective suits and visors. Women clean sinks. Men clean nuclear reactors. A dollop of ketchup on a shirt does not make a man want to suit up to get it out.

If I cleaned the house I'd want a vacuum cleaner with a motor on it, not one of these dainty supersucks. I am sick of the pitiful excuses for vacuums my wife keeps coming home with just because they're on sale and she saved fifty bucks.

One day I got off my butt and went to a Holiday Inn and asked the housekeeping chief, "What do you use every day to vacuum fifteen floors?" Turns out the answer was "industrial." They used a cross between a sandblaster and a pinball machine. It was chrome, it had rubber bumpers. The wheels were rubber, not plastic with ball bearings. It had a leather bag, not a paisley bag. You could take the bottom off this machine and see the work that had gone into it. It had a purpose. Someone thought about *using* it and not just *selling* it so that two months later you have to buy another.

I'd have bought one, but the manufacturer said I could only purchase these units in lots of a hundred—like any fine hotel. Rather than remodel my house to add a sixty-room motel wing, and hire a full-time cleaning staff, I settled for a shop vac. I'm so proud of it that I don't hide it in the closet. I leave it out. When people ask, "Where's your vacuum?" I just say, "You're sitting on it."

Men and women will do the same job in completely different ways. I don't like to wash dishes individually—as if I liked to wash them at all. I'd sooner have a sinkful of dishes and wash them all. But if I leave one unwashed dish in the sink, my wife acts as if I'd cut off her mother's arm.

She says I leave messes everywhere. I've tried to explain.

"Well I can't stop to clean up right behind my footsteps every minute. But I'll be back that way, and once the footstep is brown enough, I'll get at it."

A comic I know, Diane Ford, put it best: A woman works her ass off all the time. The guy does two things around the house and he's got to show her: "Honey, look! I fixed the screen! And look over there: I washed my dish! I put my shirt up!"

What can the wife say? "Well, why don't we put a little star on the refrigerator?"

Honestly, I don't try to get away without doing my part. I'd just rather not do it. But once you've reached a certain level of home cleanliness, it's hard to go backward. My wife is an absolute neatnik, which makes our house very pleasant to live in.

Except when I'm there.

Women depend on men to defend them, particularly from insects. If I'm in another room and hear my wife scream, I know that either some miscreant has managed to navigate our formidable security net, not to mention the surplus land mines I laid around the lot perimeter, or she's seen a trail of ants.

The last time this happened the procession ran through our bedroom all the way back into the master closet. It looked like columns of Allied troops marching into Berlin in 1945. I don't really have a problem with ants myself. They do what they do and that's okay. But for my wife's sake, I decided to encourage them to conduct their business elsewhere.

The first thing I noticed was that a couple dozen had broken off from the main group only to return with my wife's tiny $3,000 purse. It was actually kind of cute. They looked so proud. I didn't have the heart to tell them that nothing would fit inside.

An ant is a worthy opponent. It can jump a distance equal to forty times its length. And they're indestructible. You can fling them across the room—which would be like throwing me across the street—and it doesn't faze them. They just run away. And they're so stupid they don't know they can't walk upside down.

That is why I'm glad they're not the size of dogs. If they were, they could easily lift me up and carry me off. I know this because as I embarked on my mission of destruction I saw one ant running for cover, carrying a huge piece of bread. Compared to his fellow troops, he looked like the hero of the raid. He had the biggest booty, was decorated with medals, and was so excited he was going in circles, shouting, "Look at this! We'll eat for months." Back and forth. I brought my foot up. He gazed up at me. His antennae drooped. "No. Naw. No." His little ant paw went up. "Please. This is my moment. The bread . . . the children . . . my medals . . ."

Squish. Immediately a subgroup surrounded him. One was wearing robes and a cross.

I felt bad killing those ants. It was a holocaust, if you ask me. They'll be talking about this in their community for a thousand ant years. I hate thinking about the karma I've earned. But we can't live together. Sorry. So I wiped out an entire generation of ants. On the other hand, another generation will be born any minute now.

I don't like spiders either, but the more I learn about them, the more my fear turns into respect. I have not killed one purposely for a long time. I take them out in jars, leave their webs around for three or four years. What do *they* do with the webs once they're done? Do they recycle? The up side is that I've not been bitten by one lately. I think they tell each other: "Tim's okay. He could have killed a million of us. No bullshit. Did you read about the ants?"

Men's and women's magazines are very different. What's most interesting about women's publications is their preoccupation with men:

- How to tell if he's lying.
- How to stop his snoring.
- How to make him a better person.

The articles constantly emphasize a basic philosophy: If we can't live without men, let's at least try to change them.

Women get to be embarrassed, too.

- Six exercises for your love muscle.

•Sports medicine and your love muscle.

The first was actually on the cover of *Cosmo*. Helen Gurley Brown scares me.

Men's magazines do not constantly give guys advice on how to deal with her period. Or on how to stop her bullshit from getting to you. Or on how to change her.

Men's magazines reveal that men tend to mind their own business. We care about women, even celebrate them. We also celebrate the geeky guy who gets the beautiful model. But that's about as far as it goes. Men's magazines don't offer one-page quizzes to see if a couple is compatible. We don't ask if a marriage can be saved. We don't offer quick makeup tips. Men's magazines are more about fashion and getting ahead in business. I think biker magazines are the only men's publications that deal seriously with women, as in "How to make your chick look tough on your Harley."

I have some advice for women who are absorbed in women's magazines: Read a *Road and Track* now and then. Get a metallic flake-paint job and some boss rims, and maybe you'll get our attention.

Men like salty food, so you'll find us chowing down at red booth eateries like the Cock and Balls, the Cork and Cleaver, the Peach and Frog, the Slag and Bastard.

Women like anything with high-quality service. I'm not really into great service. Food is still fuel to me. The French think of food as art. Americans invented fast food. Women like restaurants where they can lunch. Women lunch. Men eat—and that's just the word you can use in polite conversation. Once, I even went to a restaurant so expensive that only the men's menu had the prices.

Of course, I only went once.

Men don't *really* like to dance. If you can drag us out onto the floor, we'll do it, but we don't like it. All dancing is to men is killing time. "When are we going home? How long do we have to do this until we can go home and do something else." Of course, there are always spoilers—guys who really get into dancing and make the rest of us look stupid.

"Look at them dance," my wife always says. She asks me all the time why we never go dancing anymore.

Why do I always have to remind her that my peg leg makes it a bit tough for me to do a carefree waltz?

We used to dance. When I was in college, discos popped up. I took *Saturday Night Fever* so seriously I even bought a white suit. At the time I had no idea that the seventies would turn out to be the cheesiest, most garish of all eras. Neck chains and more neck chains.

We learned to dance in groups. It was almost like country-music line dancing now. It was a great time. Instead of drinking or causing trouble, we danced. We'd come out of the club at two in the morning, sweaty, ready to sleep.

Not everyone was into disco. There were still poetry houses where many women went and talked, sang, and thought about silent desperation. But the rest of us, tired of the struggles of the sixties, just wanted to whoop it up before the eighties arrived and we had to make tons of money. We knew there was enough time for desperation later. We wanted to party while we were still too dense to realize how stupid we looked in Partridge family fashions.

Got a second? I have a couple of fantasies I'm dying to share. I'm sure no woman's ever had this fantasy, which just goes to show you once again how different we are.

I want Scottish bodyguards, Ian and Ion and Ogor, dressed in kilts. Each would weigh three hundred pounds. We'd go to functions and these guys would say, "Aye! You gotta get back, laddie! Timmy's coming through!"

I also wonder, just for a goof, what would happen if I had tits. A guy like me, just so I could go to the beach and make my friends uncomfortable.

"God, Tim, man, you got some nice tits."

And you can't really tell me to put a top on, because I'm a guy. I could walk around, take off my shirt, go into a garage. The mechanic would say, "God, you got nice tits! Has anybody ever said that? I don't know how else to say it. I'm not gay, but man, you got some *tits*. Nice tits."

I don't know why I brought that up.

As we know, even though men call it bullshitting, men just out and out lie.

One reason men lie so much is that we get forced into it. It's the truth! Our lying increases the longer we're married because our mates ask us to do such ridiculous things. They're always suggesting changes in our behavior. In their realm, behavioral changes suggested by occasional lunch partners supposedly help women get better. To men it sounds like, "Are you trying to tell me what to do?"

For instance, women like to send thank-you notes. Women send thank-you notes for thank-you notes. "Thank you for that thank-you note, where did you get it? Let's have lunch and talk about our thank-you notes."

A thank-you note? Wait a minute, it was a gift, wasn't it? The Bible says you give freely. You give a gift, that's it. You don't want a Hansel-and-Gretel note back saying, "Thanks, I got it." This is a female ritual. They nag their husbands to do it, too.

"Send a thank-you note."

"I don't want to."

"Send a goddamn thank-you note."

"I don't want to."

"You send the damn thing, they're your friends."

Pretty soon a guy will say, "All right, All right, just stop yelling at me!" So you start lying, and so begins the routine: bitch, lie, bitch, lie, bitch, lie.

"Okay, I'll send one!" He's thinking: "I'm not sending anything."

Has it always been like that? Cro-Magnon man? Neolithic times? Valley Gwanda. Grog having a big dinner. Unngghh. Later, a shrill cry from the woman: "Hey, who took a dump in the cave?"

"Who took a dump in the cave?" You know a man is about to lie when he repeats the question. It gives him a moment to think about it. These days it's no different.

"Honey, where's the Crockpot?"

"Our Crockpot?"

"No, the Pope's Crockpot."

"That'd be in Italy, wouldn't it?" Always be a smart-ass if you can, because it'll take her mind off the original question. Men have to lie to get women off their backs.

Because women rely on a communication network, they abhor lying. Oh, they *do* it as well as men, but they hate it because it destroys the fabric of trust. Men know that, which is why they often call their lies bullshitting.

"Your grandfather *did not* leg wrestle with Mussolini."

"He was just bullshitting."

I have a friend who I don't believe has *ever* told the truth. Obviously the guy wasn't a tank squadron commander in World War Two, but if that helps his story along, what the hell? Sometimes he gets so immersed in these tales that, after describing his foray behind German lines, he'll also say, "And then, when I went to Vietnam . . ."

Even I wouldn't want to defend that kind of bullshitting.

This kind of bullshit happens everywhere, even in publishing. Ever read *The Celestine Prophecy*, a bunch of New Age homilies disguised as a travelogue? Carlos Castaneda had something he wanted to tell us, but he knew we wouldn't believe it if he just told it to some professor at Cal State. So he made up this elaborate fiction. Is it lying? Bullshit? (Lawyers and actors make a living like this.) I think all three are the same.

This is probably why, no matter how many times I tell my wife I've been on the space shuttle, she doesn't believe me.

Live with a woman for only five minutes, and any man will realize that each sex perceives the world in a completely different way, despite sharing the same five senses. Women are hypersensitive to many things, and dull as a brick to others. And they would say the same about us.

I can hear a machine bearing going out from about a mile away. I live in a big house, and once I could "feel" that the compressor on the furnace wasn't functioning correctly. I kept saying, "What is that noise?"

My wife said, "What noise?"

"Can't you hear it? Ack, ack, ack, ack, ack, ack . . ."

Finally she said, "Well . . . Suzie cleaned the furnace yesterday."

Cleaned the furnace! I knew it. I raced to the basement, took one look at the furnace, and it was obvious that somehow the insulation was torn off the filter. It was hanging down into the fan, making the fan very heavy on one side, which burnt out the bearing and made it chirp like a little bird in a big cat's mouth. Had it continued it would have frozen up and the furnace would have blown sky high and everyone would have died in an inferno hotter than the surface of the sun.

I'm not bullshitting. It's a good thing I was around to detect the problem. Even if my wife had heard the bearing, she would no more have taken the access panel off the furnace than anyone else in their right mind. But I removed it because once you get inside things aren't that difficult to figure out. And once I got back from the hospital, I was sure that that was not the thing I should have touched.

Women have a problem with loud and soft. There's no sense buying a stereo with a woman in the house. The volume is never low enough unless it's off, unless they're drinking with their girlfriends.

"Honey? Turn that song up. I like that."

And then when her consciousness returns, "God, it's loud in here!"

"You asked me to turn it up a minute ago."

I hate the volume so low that I can hear my breathing.

The worst part is trying to watch TV late at night, in bed. Everything is always too loud. Not just the TV, which *does* tend to vary drastically in volume as I surf through the channels. I can't read either. Turning the page makes too much noise. I'd fart, but she might bolt up, half asleep, and dial 911.

I finally got a remote headset and solved the problem.

Now the flickering screen bothers her. Light, dark, light, dark. I thought people slept with their eyes *closed.*

I think my wife is sending me a message. "Either go to sleep at the same time, or do your stuff in the living room."

Women are always cold. Chilly. "She's got a chill. Are you chilly? I'm a little chilly."

Men never even use the word. "I'm freezing my butt off! Okay?"

My wife says I'm clammy. We're in bed and she's going, "You're warm. You're clammy. I'm chilly. Isn't it a little chilly in here?"

I've always got a little sweat going, so there's not much I can do about it. Thank goodness they've now got cars that have smart dual thermostats. I keep my side cold and her side warm. She'd rather have the whole car warm just to make me uncomfortable, but that's a control thing.

If you want to see what I mean about these temperature differentials, try taking a bath with a woman. You could boil fish in a woman's bathwater. You've got to use your balls as a thermometer and do Sumo wrestler deep knee bends to see if your jewels get too warm. By the time you're in, the water's lukewarm, and she's out.

My wife and I were in a Miami hotel once, trying to sleep, but running wind sprints to the room thermostat instead. When I finally turned it off it was 98 degrees. This was the middle of summer. Maximum humidity. It was so damn hot that I looked like I had malaria. I had a glaze on and there were yellow flies circling my head. I had to have a big bottle of quinine next to the bed.

Meanwhile, she's got the comforter up around her neck, going, "Are you chilly at all?"

I said, "Look at me. I've got cracked lips, I've got that desert pallor." I looked horrible. Turns out she was chilled because she had her period. As we know, a man can't understand that unless he's in a woman's body.

So don't even try.

There's not a woman reading this book who's ever had her butt sticking in the air and a flame shooting out of it. This is a primary difference between women and men. Men will actually *light a fart*. Yes, I know you women are saying, "Wait, wait!" But it's true. Ask your husband.

Women don't think of things like this. I've known my wife twelve years and she hasn't ever farted, much less blown a torch out of her butt. At least, not that I know of. I don't ask her to tell me when it happens, either, but you'd think once every few years you'd hear a noise. And you *know* women don't say to other women, "Helen, come over here, pull my finger."

Can you imagine women lighting farts?

"Uh, Janet? Put a cap in it. This is a bridge club, not a refinery."

Women never go out of the house with a booger in their nose, either. Think about it. You've never seen it. I always have boogers in my nose. Before important meetings my wife says, "Tim . . ."

"What? Oh oh." How do you miss a booger as big as a moose? Simple. I don't look in the mirror. I've got whiteheads, hairs growing out of my ears, and my wife is just like a baboon, plucking and pulling at me.

"Get away!"

Women are always looking at themselves in the mirror. Men look once in a while. We get about five feet away, angle ourselves till we find a position that looks pretty cool, and that's it. Men as a rule think they're far better looking than they are. Women, as a rule, think they're far uglier than they really are. Men find a pose and freeze: "I look pretty goddamn good at that angle!" This is one reason bald guys can even walk out of the house. Angles.

Women squint about a millimeter from the mirror and find stuff that dermatologists don't even want to look at. Squeezing, popping, fidgeting. They come out of the bathroom looking like you beat 'em up! They've got little blue marks all over their faces.

"How do I look?"

I want to say, "You look like hell." But you tell them that and it causes another zit, so it's "Yeah, you look great."

Women don't believe you anyway. Not when they've got mirrors that make their nose hairs look like timbers.

Women don't burp, either: "Hey Helen, blaaaaat!"

Men are chronic burpers. My brother has turned it into an Olympic event. One Thanksgiving he did a blow burp across the table, just a "bluuuuuhhhh."

"Oh, man. Was that you? Good one! I think you knocked Grandma in the soup with that one. Yup, she's down!"

And women don't learn how to spit. Men have to get their hawking act together early. You can't graduate to manhood otherwise. I'd love to see my Gram and Aunt Rose burping and spitting.

"My, my, that cheese ring was rich, wasn't it?"

"Phhhttt."

Sometimes a man can learn something important from a woman.

I came in early one night from watching a Monday-night football game at a friend's. The ladies were in the house gathered in front of a Discovery Channel special on breast cancer. I didn't know what they were doing. I just saw breasts being groped.

"Yeah. You gals are a little hipper than I thought."

You idiot!

Pretty quickly I had to sit there and shut up and learn about breast cancer. They say that if women, starting at age thirty-five, had a, breast exam about once a year, breast cancer would be reduced by forty percent. I think one problem is that men don't realize how degrading the examination is for women. Have you ever seen a mammogram machine? It's like a drill press for tits.

"Hey, hey, hey! Get it outta there!"

I don't think a woman designed this machine. I'm glad they don't do penograms.

Or do they?

I don't want to know. The prostate exam is bad (and necessary) enough.

The things that women will go through to make themselves beautiful for their boyfriends and husbands amazes me. Plucking their eyebrows. Bikini waxing. Ripping hair right off their crotches. This is something you will never see a man doing. That ball hair is staying right where it is. Even though we all gotta admit that ball hair is the ugliest spot on the planet Earth. There's not a woman alive who hasn't been scared to death of her husband naked bent over a bathtub. She wanders in and . . . "AAAAAAHHHH! . . . Oh, it's you. I thought a wildebeest had wandered in here or something. Honey, I love you, I really do, but I don't ever want to see that again!"

There's something I want to make perfectly clear—now that Richard Nixon is gone, that phrase is up for grabs, isn't it? Dibs!—before I get into big trouble. It's a misnomer to call anybody "yours." Throughout this book, I'm always saying "My wife."

Laura is not *my* wife. She's just *nobody else's* wife.

"Hi, I'm Tim, and this is nobody else's wife, Laura."

❙ don't want to be flippant about this. This is a philosophical problem that strikes to the heart of the matter. It epitomizes the differences between men and women, between ideological groups, even countries. One way or another this is at the heart of all arguments: Seat up or seat down?

"Remember to put the seat down after you're done."

"Why? Do you put the seat up after *you're* done?"

"Just put it down."

"Why?"

Trust me, women will come up with a reason.

"It looks better down. It's gotta be down."

"Yeah? Then I've always got to lift it up, or I dribble on the seat . . ."

"Well, if you leave it down," says my wife, "then I've got to sit on it."

Look, I can understand that in the middle of the night a woman doesn't like to accidentally fall into the can when the last thing she's thinking about is whether the seat is up or down.

But why is it my responsibility to put it down anymore than it's hers to put it up? I sit down, too, now and then.

Okay, okay. If seats were meant to be up, why would they make lids in the first place? All right? Is my macho withering before your eyes? The normal position is with the lid down. You don't leave car doors open so the next time you can just step right in.

But seat up/seat down speaks to a larger issue: Who is right, and who is wrong?

Speaking from a male perspective, it seems men are always wrong. Naturally wrong. Women will joke about it, like, "Yes, you are, ha-ha-ha," but women come from the position that they're right anyway and we're always wrong to begin with. They laugh it off, "Don't let it bother you. It's really just part of your charm."

Of course, the point of this book has been to have fun with those differences; have fun and move on.

the secrets
men never
tell women

Do I look stupid? Why do you think they're called secrets?

the family of man

Have a kid and everything changes. This will not be news to most of you, but it was news to me. Big news. I had heard those words over and over, and still I couldn't have anticipated the consequences. No one could have accurately described them to me, even though lots of people tried.

I'd like to share them.

And since this is my book and not yours, you'll just have to put up with my going on about this for a while. Or else I'm taking my bottles and diapers and going home, to put myself down for a nap.

See. Have a kid, and right away you start acting like one.

We never tried to get pregnant. It just kind of happened. We knew we wanted kids, as a concept, but the lunatics inside both my wife and me were still scared, and maybe a bit selfish. It took us eight years even to get married. I thought, "What would I do with a kid? What would a kid do with me?"

And then, one night, within a moment, my whole perspective changed. I was staying with an old friend from childhood, and her father was in town. We were sitting in her living room, laughing about something, and suddenly I noticed her father looking at her with what can only be described (though words cannot really describe the look) as a sparkling gaze of pride, love, and friendship. All at once he asked for a kiss and a hug. I said, "I'll hug you, but a kiss is out of the question." I learned later that he was speaking to her.

This ineffable moment between parent and child made me rethink everything. We knew—superficially—that having a child would change our lives, change sex, change everything.

Guess what? It's the best thing that ever happened to us. We wouldn't change a thing.

My reaction to the news that Laura was pregnant was screaming. Loud, sustained screaming.

My wife said, "Is something wrong?"

"No, no. That's an excited scream." Nuances can be so subtle.

In retrospect, the whole process was kind of fun. I've never had such manly feelings, both for her as well as about myself. Laura has never looked more radiant. There's something about how lovely pregnant women are that even makes you fall in love with pregnant strangers.

Of course, we were scared to death. Laura said, "Now what do we do?" We worried: "Oh, God, what if the baby doesn't make it? What if it's sick or deformed?" The terror is nonstop, even after they're born. *Mostly* after they're born.

When I got the news that we were expecting, I called my older brother and asked for his advice. He said, "I'd suggest going out to dinner."

"That's all you can tell me about having a kid?"

"I'm telling you: just pick a place *right now* and go out to dinner, because you will not be able to do this for a long, long time, and you don't realize how cool it is just to go out to dinner. Even if you have a baby-sitter, it's almost unbearable the first time the kid stands at the door as you're trying to get into the car, crying wildly because he or she doesn't want you to go out. Try and enjoy your dinner *then*."

How much being a parent would change my life didn't occur to me until I was heaving up my dinner the day my daughter was born. I'd had dinner at the hospital, then had to stop in the parking lot and throw up: once because of the baby, twice because of the food. When I finally got home, my first instinct was to pack a suitcase, leave a note—"I can't handle this"—and run away.

Before my daughter was born, we learned that she had a potential genetic defect. It's a horror that a lot of people go through. I understand it. Our doctor was very concerned. A specialist said, "It's within normal values for this certain enzyme, but it's on the edge."

Everything worked out okay.

During the tests, our doctor had a picture of my daughter's chromosomes on the wall.

"Well, there she is. You must be very proud."

"God, she looks so . . . small."

"All those rods are what will determine her every detail."

So I asked if there was a way we could give her bigger tits. The doctor took me seriously.

"No!"

"What about better eyesight?"

She got really mad. "You can't go in there and start fiddling with your child's chromosomes, young man!" With that, my wife and I took our chromosomes and left. Later, Laura told me the doctor wanted to test me, as well. Before our appointment, Laura kept reminding me to wear clean underwear.

"Are they clean?"

"I don't know."

"What do you mean you don't know? How can you not know?"

"They were clean when they originally started, but I went to the gym today and I've been running around."

Laura explained that the doctor was going to want to see my penis. That sounded like a reasonable request. Besides, I'd been wanting to show it to her. Not really. In fact, quite the opposite. I felt very uncomfortable. Every time the doctor would ask me a question, I got pissy.

Finally, I said, "Enough with the questions. When do I get to show you my penis!" The doctor said nothing.

Then Laura piped up. "Sorry, doctor. He's like this with *everybody*." Then they both started laughing.

I discovered later that the two of them were in on this and just trying to get back at me for that crack about the chromosomes.

I had to kill them both.

My next book will be about single parenting.

It was a natural birth. That is, there were no Satanists in the delivery room. We used the Lamaze method. Look at the word closely. With a little male ingenuity, a well-positioned apostrophe, and French as a second language, Lamaze could be rewritten as L'Amaze. That's what birth is. Amazing.

At the time, though, I kept thinking it was LaFromage, or LaDécoupage, or something like that.

My wife didn't want her drugs until after our daughter was born. I told her, "This is not the Olympics or a gladiator movie. If it starts hurting, take the damn Demerol."

That, and a stern look at the attending nurse, and I didn't have to say it twice.

My wife was really good. We'd gone to childbirth classes together and she wanted me there. She could have cussed out the nurses when the pain got too intense, but it wouldn't have meant as much to her as cursing someone who would take it personally.

It's a good thing I was around. Laura was breathing all wrong and the baby started coming out before it was ready. I had to remind her to hold on.

"Honey. Honey. Hold your breath. We've got to wait until the doctor putts out on the eighteenth green."

Before my kid was born, I used to think very differently about being in the delivery room. Like: There's absolutely no reason to be around. You're there for support, but you're really just a pain in the ass. You coo and whisper supportively, trying to help your wife concentrate on her breathing. It never works.

If it was me having the kid, I'd want to hear a manly song I could sing along with: "In 1814, we took a little trip, along with Colonel Jackson, down the mighty Mississip. We took a little bacon and we took a little beans . . ." I could breathe to the drum cadence.

Men also say such stupid things in the delivery room. Men are such lamebrains. She's lying there, and we're going, "God, honey, that's gotta hurt," or "Will I be able to use that area again?"

DON'T STAND TOO CLOSE TO A NAKED MAN

The woman is also angry, but she's drugged up, tied down, and what the hell is she going to do about it?

You've got a take your licks when you can.

"I don't like your cooking all that well, either. *Honey.* And you look like hell on Sunday morning."

But that attitude changed the minute we got into the birthing room. I gained considerable insight and realized that birth has a deeper meaning for men than we suspect. Seeing the process first-hand just reinforced my belief that men are far more jealous about women's ability to bear a child than we'll admit. Men can build a skyscraper, but we can't hug it, feed it, change it, coach its Little League team, teach it about sex, or spring it from jail when it's caught joyriding in the family station wagon at three in the morning.

I've read that men are like bees; they just hover around the uterus trying to reproduce themselves. I've also heard that men come out of women and spend the rest of their lives trying to get back in. I don't think it's very complex. The whole business of men and women is reproduction; there's nothing else to it. All the arguments, all the horseshit, all the rhetoric is, at bottom, about reproduction. We can't do what women can, so they have the ultimate power. We act like they don't. We treat them horribly because we can't have kids. We demean them—not because they'll accept it, but just to keep them in their place. If women understood the power they have, I don't know what we'd do.

Maybe they *do* know. Nah, I can't even consider that. Too scary.

I can't even fathom having a kid. I watched that child come out. The pride swelled up in me. Also the anger, and the competition. What I witnessed was something that hurt my woman and I couldn't stop it. And something that made her happy in a way that I've never been able to make her happy.

This doesn't mean her screams didn't make me think, "Boy! I'm glad I'm a guy!"

That's right. I'm not sorry I'm a man. True, men have all of the destructive tendencies. We're encouraged to be little destroyers from birth. These traits come in handy, though. Once we have a family, we'll destroy anything we have to that threatens it. Women like us for that. Sometimes men get so confused they actually destroy the family.

Some men want to understand pregnancy so desperately (or just get their wives to shut up when their ankles swell to the size of holiday cheese logs) that they'll strap on one of those fake bellies and walk around for a while. This is going a little too far. If you're going to write about it so that we all understand it, okay. It's like *Black Like Me*. But if you just want to find out what it's like to weigh eighty pounds more, you can eat a lot of those cheese logs or make a movie like *The Santa Clause*.

An odd thing about fatherhood is the change in camaraderie with other male parents, especially when your kids are still very small. You bond, but the adhesion principle is altogether different from the stereotypical macho posturing about one's fertility and already being able to pay for the kid's college education. That went out long ago, with the eighties. This bond is rife with genuine tenderness, vulnerability, and a little sadness. I don't know why. It just is— maybe because having a kid finally connects a man to something he loves unconditionally that, unlike his car or power tools, can actually love him in return.

One guy I know is afraid that someday somebody wearing a suit and carrying a gun is going to walk up to him, out of a crowd, and simply say, "We know. We know you don't know what you're doing. We've been monitoring you." I know what he means. It's not really the "monitors," it's the reality police. It seems like my whole life has been by the seat of my pants. I'm making it up as I go along. I find it strangely funny that God allows me to make decisions; that life *does* just unfold, and lets me do the best I can. This particularly applies to fatherhood, in which you have ultimate responsibility for a totally dependent being. You can't go back and redo stuff you did, but you can't know if you're getting it right the first time, either.

There are some rules, however.

"Don't go near the pool. Don't hit me in the stomach. You've got to eat more." I just want to take care of my daughter. I don't want her sick. I'm worried about her falling.

My wife is far better at this teaching stuff than I am. She thinks she's horrible at it, but she's wrong. That is why she can bask unashamedly in the delight of the school's calling to say, "Your child is doing extremely well in fire prevention. And the drop drill. Also, your daughter seems to know military rules quite well. She salutes. What are you doing with her at home?"

Working so much, I feel oddly distant from the whole process. I do what I can. There's a lot of guilt involved. My wife says, "If you spent more time with her . . ." I spend all the time I can with her. I'm getting better at it, though. Rather than read aloud from books on military tactics and supply requisitioning, we go to dinner and have a couple of kiddy cocktails and a marvelous time. This is usually when Mommy isn't around. My little girl and I relate better then. They're alone together so much. We're alone so rarely. When we're alone together, she and I somehow behave differently. We learn about each other. She learns that I'm her father. I learn that she's my daughter. It's a weird feeling, but any parent knows what I'm talking about when I say that I often look at my daughter and wonder just whose kid she is. Where'd she suddenly come from? And why on earth did she pick Laura and me for parents?

When my daughter and I are alone she'll hug my leg and say, "I just love you so much, Daddy!" She's so used to my leaving that when I tell her she and I are going to hang out all night, she gets this great look on her face and says, "We've got *so much* to do, Dad!" There's nothing like it in the world.

I want my relationship with my daughter to keep growing, so I've been giving my wife a couple of hundred bucks each week and making her go to the mall with her girlfriends, or something—anything!

But this closeness is not without its problems. When I'm sitting there playing with Barbie, washing her hair, the lunatic in me suddenly says, *I've got to get a scotch and get the hell outta . . .* Right in the middle of all this pleasantness, the lunatic goes, *Look at yourself! You're bathing dolls!*

My daughter likes to bathe with me. She goes, "Jac*uuu*zi!" and gets scared when I put the jets on. She likes them, but wants me in there with her. I've *got* to be there. But I need to know: When do you stop bathing with your daughter? There's a day. It's coming. I want to mark my calendar. Oprah must know. Phil must know. Geraldo must . . . nah. I keep asking around, because I never want to find out I've missed it by a day, but I keep getting this: "Oh, you'll know."

I'm not so sure. I want to cut it off long before *you'll know*, whatever *you'll know* is. Sounds like an est seminar. I don't want another situation like my brothers and me seeing my mom in the shower and staring just a moment too long.

My daughter likes me to chase her—definitely a girl thing that stays with them until the day when they finally allow some lucky guy to catch them. I'm teaching her early, though, to run real fast. I like it better when we're working on my car. I drag her into my world whenever I can. She wanted to help me paint the raised letters on my tires. She likes going for rides with me. She loves going fast. She thinks my Mustang is a Ferrari. That's probably not a bad thing. If I'm real lucky, it will probably save me some money when she wants a Ferrari for her sixteenth birthday.

Having a kid has made me do things I never imagined I would. I nurture *other* people's kids. I used to be such a smart-ass around other people who had kids when I didn't. And now, no matter what they do, I understand. I can be talking to an adult and wiping snot off his kid's mouth. I'm grabbing boogers out of some kid's nose and wiping them underneath the table or on the couch. Hey—either I do it, or he will.

My wife and I used to avoid sitting next to people with small children on an airplane. Then, the worst thing in the world was a screaming baby.

"Can't they take care of the kid and stop it from crying? Give it something! Why don't they sit in the back of the plane with the engine noise? With a couple of oxygen masks and a blanket, I don't see why they can't ride in the baggage compartment. At least until he stops crying. We paid for these seats!" Like they didn't. Like they get them free. (Don't beleaguered parents always look like indigents even if they're rich?) They're hiding the child and saying "Sorry" to the whole plane, like "Forgive me for having this baby!" We didn't mean to interrupt you reading your inflight magazine.

But once it's your kid, you look at anyone who's impatient with you like, "What's the matter with *you*? How come you don't have a kid? Get with the program and join the family of man!"

Every single thing you thought you'd never say or think, you say and think in the first two months after childbirth. Everything.

Now I yearn for a better life for *all* children. I'm interested in better education systems. In mentoring. In health care and eliminating ketchup from consideration as a vegetable at lunch. (Thanks, Ronald Reagan.) It's brought my whole life into focus. And yet, now and then, the lunatic will say, "Uh huh, right! You could run them both over, take the money you got from the TV show, and live with some island beauties, drinking lime rickeys in the Bahamas!"

The lunatic is still alive. Now he just has nowhere near the impact. Besides, I can't hear him as well with the kid crying.

When you're raising kids, it's valuable to have listened to your parents when you were young. You hope they listened to their parents, too. Passing childrearing wisdom from generation to generation becomes very important. For instance, "You can't party your ass off all your life." You can, but eventually you realize it's energy misdirected.

When my attitude was bad, as a kid, my mom used to say, "I can't wait until you have your own kid." Yeah, right.

"It'll be *all different* when I have my own kid," I'd say. I was an idiot. Parents wait for that day. And they love to rub it in.

Now, how many times have I said, "Who put this bike here?" when I know exactly who put the bike there.

"Who put boogers on the wall? Who's wiping the boogers all over the wall!"

During one Christmas my daughter went through this phase

where she'd pick her nose and wipe it anywhere. My wife, like a real smart parent, said, "You know, you can eat those things!"

At least my wife wasn't wiping stuff on the wall.

Swearing too much around the house is also dangerous when there's a young child about. I've said stuff, then realized my daughter was listening. Even in general conversation you've got to be careful. Kids are a lot like celebrities. Even though they're in the room, people talk about them as if they aren't. You make decisions about and for the child, and you forget they can hear you. They're not stupid. And then, when you're least expecting it, they become little myna birds and repeat what you say.

Recently, my daughter and I went to the supermarket, but not the same market her mom takes her to. She goes there because there are generally fewer people there at a certain time of the day. I don't shop, but I had to get something for dinner, because I'd said I'd make dinner. On the way there, my daughter said, "This isn't where Mommy goes."

"I know, but it's where we're going."

And she said, "Ugh! It'll be a slow boat to China before you can get through that line in a hurry!"

Life's so unfair. Carol died. That's my daughter's fish. We tried to explain death to her. She cried when she found Carol just floating there. We wouldn't have wanted her to see it, but we realized she had to start somewhere and it might as well be with the fish that my wife murdered! Hey, I'm not pointing fingers, but she did spray insecticide in the room, which got in the water, which aced the fish. We were all pretty sad, especially me. I took care of Carol. I liked that fish. This fish had even made it through the big Los Angeles earthquake. It was two hours before we noticed her on the carpet. What a trouper. I would have done anything to save that fish long after my kid got bored with it.

But the fish was dead.

We said we could bury her. I tried to explain that people don't last forever, either. My daughter seemed to understand and accept this. Then, for two weeks, all I heard was *"You're* going to die, but Mommy's not going to." This always made me very happy to hear.

I said, "No, we both will die."

"No! Not Mommy, but *you.* You can die, but Mommy's not going to die." Always ready with a quick comeback, I said, "Don't make me prove it."

I'll admit it. When we did the first ultrasound and they said, "It's a little girl," I went, "Ohhh." I actually made that sound. Like I'd opened the wrong Christmas present. Three people in the room said, "What was *that* all about?" My wife said, "What's 'Ohhh' for?"

"Oh—hrmph—I was clearing my throat. Oh, look! A girl! Ohhhh! Dresses and parties and a friend to you! Look at that!"

I was very disappointed. And now, of course, I feel guilty in front of God. This girl is so much pleasure to me that it's incredible. I go to other guys' houses, and their boys are little monsters. The difference is night and day.

Girls love dolls. In a boy's room, if there's a doll, it has no head. Boys love cars. My daughter has car models because I'm trying, very, very slowly, to teach her to tell a Mustang from a Ferrari. I bought her a model that cost *fifty dollars*! I said, "It's really cool." A few weeks later I asked her where it was. She brought it to me. All the mirrors were broken off. But she likes it. She carries it around with her in her purse. Something's very wrong when a little girl carries a model Volkswagen around in her purse. It's in there with a troll doll and some lipstick. It was supposed to be in its little case. She doesn't care about that. It's jewelry to her.

I'm not sure what this means, but I'm already worried.

When I sit back on a warm night, caressed by a soft breeze, sipping a glass of wine, and I see my daughter playing in the yard, I stop for a moment and think, "There's a lot of pain coming."

As she grows up she's going to hurt me, without even wanting to. She already hurts me and doesn't know how much.

Love hurts.

Once again, I've learned what I've always known: Women are very important for so many different reasons. I don't have to learn this from my daughter, but I'll have to put up with it from her. And maybe I can also pass on to her some understanding of men.

Men don't come from the place of anger or superiority that women think we do. We come from a culture of our own that's based on certain rules and regulations about how men live. I don't read it as power over women, but women think that we do.

Man will always be an outsider, no matter how much he stays at home, cooks, cleans, irons, vacuums, nurtures. I've worn an apron for about six months now. It hasn't done the job. But I'm sticking with the spike heels.

What I'd like my daughter to be is everything her mother is but with some of my input. I wasn't around for my wife's upbringing. I can't change her, even though I might sometimes want to. I'm in on the bottom floor with my daughter. Of course, she's already a lot like her mother, only more hyper and emotional. And shorter. Anyway, I already know I'm not going to be able to change her either. Deep down I'm not sure I really want to.

Having a child has really changed my relationship with my wife. We appreciate our time together more. I love her more than I ever have because she's brought this wonderful thing into my life and she's turned out to be a marvelous mother. We can't argue as much, though, because we don't want our child to hear it.

Instead, we'll clench our teeth and hiss, "Just smile, then."

We never smiled this much when we argued before.

One problem is that when we do argue, my daughter always blames me. Is that the lesson? Girls always stick together?

We're a family, which is the beautiful thing. We're different now. My daughter writes letters in school that say, "I love my mommy. I love my daddy. I love that we're a family." And I'm beginning to love it. I'm beginning to love the three of us doing things together. I love the dynamic we have. I wish I had three children already. I wish two were a lot older. Then Laura and I could give them the responsibility for raising the youngest and we could sit on the patio drinking lime rickeys at sunset.

Being a family has gotten our relationship more in tune. We're part of the family of man. My daughter is only four and a half, but already I love our conversations. I love when she asks me questions about life.

I hope my daughter stays interested in the family and doesn't get so involved in school that I never see her. (Yeah, right.) Or that she doesn't one day say, "Ugh, my parents are taking me to Italy. I wish I could stay at home and just hang out." (Good luck!) And I really hope she never tells anyone, "My father is *such* a pain. I wish I could figure him out."

On second thought, maybe I *wouldn't* mind that.

AFTERWORD:
men and their tools

All of my life I have wrestled with men's penchant for destruction. But I have also admired our ability to re-create what has been destroyed. The ability of men to create is in many ways and at many times the very best of us. Of course, we can't create the way women can, and that truth has a profound effect on men, at many levels. At worst, we experience feelings of uselessness, mistrust, even hostility. At best, we long to protect, provide, and create.

The creations of men are wonderful things to behold. Just watch a man build a race engine, tie a fly rod. Overlook for the moment that we can also create the most fiendish weapons. Observe the painter at work, the mason building. That's why tools are wonderful, that's why shop class is wonderful. When men are building they're not threatening. When men do not threaten, they nurture and maintain their creations. This is something I hope women understand. There's much to learn about the male animal, particularly through the things we make.

Go to a hot-rod show. If you haven't been, just go once. I know, I know: Lots of women don't like hot-rod shows. But go and you will see what turns men on. You will see the details. Look under one of these cars. See how it's polished and chromed. It's so clean. And colorful. Yet it's the *underside* of a car.

Whatever man does, he can undo. Whatever we have destroyed we can re-create. Whatever we've created badly we can remodel. What we've forgotten we can relearn. This is the genius in man.

Men don't need to be tamed. We just need to be listened to just like women. We need to be left alone now and then, just like women. Men have some class, too.

And now excuse me, I've got to take a leak.

I'll try to remember to put the seat down afterward.

Thanks for reading.